I AM A CHRISTIAN

I · AM · A CHRISTIAN

Authentic Accounts of Christian Martyrdom
and Persecution from the Ancient Sources

compiled and edited by
Anthony P. Schiavo, Jr.

Arx Publishing
Merchantville, New Jersey

Arx Publishing
Merchantville, New Jersey

I Am A Christian:
Authentic Accounts of Christian Martyrdom
and Persecution from the Ancient Sources

©2018 Arx Publishing, LLC
All Rights Reserved

First Edition

ISBN: 978-1-935228-18-9

To Helen

A most excellent daughter and unfailing helper.

Table of Contents

Preface ix
Introduction xiii

Chapter 1: The First Martyrs 3
Chapter 2: The Passion of Saint Ignatius of Antioch 17
Chapter 3: The Passion of Saint Polycarp 25
Chapter 4: The Passion of Justin Martyr and Companions 37
Chapter 5: The Apology and Acts of Apollonius 43
Chapter 6: The Scillitan Martyrs 51
Chapter 7: The Passion of Saints Perpetua, Felicitas and Companions ... 55
Chapter 8: Saints Potamiena, Basilides and the Pupils of Origen
   who Became Martyrs 73
Chapter 9: The Martyrs of Alexandria during the Decian Persecution ... 77
Chapter 10: The Passion of Saint Saturninus 85
Chapter 11: The Martyrdom of Saint Cyprian 93
Chapter 12: The Martyrdom of Saint Lawrence 103
Chapter 13: The Passion of Saint Fructuosus of Tarragona and Companions ... 109
Chapter 14: The Acts of Saints Chionia, Agape, and Irene
   Who Hid the Scriptures 115
Chapter 15: "Traditores" and the Burning of Christian Books 123
Chapter 16: The Martyrs of Abitina 129
Chapter 17: The Passion of Saint Crispina 139
Chapter 18: Saint Agnes of Rome 143
Chapter 19: Martyrdom Poems of Prudentius 149
Chapter 20: The Persian Martyrs 159
Chapter 21: Martyrs during the Reign of Julian the Apostate 171

Appendix: The Epitaphs of Pope Saint Damasus 179

Sources 191

Index 193

Preface

We live in an age when a vast amount of information is available within seconds to anyone seeking it. For the lover of history, this means that even the most obscure figure or event may be thoroughly researched with relative ease. However, the sheer mass of information—much of it invalid or inaccurate—often results in confusion and error, particularly for readers without the time, energy or expertise to properly sift through it.

Though varying in scope, a problem similar to this existed in antiquity. When Christianity began to spread throughout the ancient Roman world, an insatiable demand for literature relating to Christ, the Apostles and the earliest saints erupted among the newly-Christianized. Fascinated by their new faith, the catechumens wanted details about their predecessors who had suffered and died decades or centuries before. To obtain this information, ancient legal records—which the Romans meticulously kept—were investigated. In several cases, the transcripts of the actual trials of martyrs and confessors were discovered. These precious records formed the seed of early Christian hagiographical literature that would flower during the 5th century AD and beyond.

In later centuries, such fascinating Acts and Passions of the ancient martyrs became so popular that a cottage industry sprang up devoted to generating them in great numbers. Many of these tales, though containing a kernel of truth, were padded by later writers who wished to make them more dramatic or to emphasize a particular theological point of the moment. Others were blatant works of fiction written to fill a perceived gap in a particular saint's biography.

Sadly, these fabulous, fictional or semi-fictional works have come to define the genre. As a result, many modern students are never exposed to the invaluable diamonds that exist among the debris. Indeed, many are taught that because some early Christian literature has been subject to later additions and embellishment, that the whole field is untrustworthy and therefore untrue.

The works included in the present volume are a few of the diamonds—accounts considered authentic even by the most skeptical scholars. Taken together, they form an authentic record of early Christian zeal and fortitude in the face of aggressive state persecution. They retain much of the force and inspirational value for present-day Christians as they did for ancient converts. When reading them, you will notice a common refrain: when accused of any crime, the courageous defendants would cry out: "I am a Christian" which was the equivalent of saying, "I am guilty as charged."

These relic works are particularly valuable because they are survivors. As the reader will see in Chapters 14, 15, and 16 of the present volume, the Sacred Scriptures and all works of Christian literature were condemned to be burned during the early 4th century empire-wide persecution of the Roman emperors Diocletian and Galerius. Many such works were consigned to the flames during this period, as demonstrated dramatically in Chapter 15. Attempting to hide and protect them could result in torture and death, as was inflicted upon Saints Chionia, Agape and Irene in Chapter 14 and the martyrs of Abitina in Chapter 16.

The purpose of this book is to allow the authentic voices of the early Christians to ring out clearly again with as little interpretation as possible. For this reason, I have attempted to keep commentary to a minimum, letting it suffice to set the scene for each chapter and offering pathways to additional research which the reader may pursue if he or she is so inclined. Most of the accounts included in this book are taken from 19th century English translations and are displayed here in a roman typeface. My own attempts at adding historical narrative to help enhance the context of the ancient passages are shown in an italic font so that the original source material may stand out more clearly.

Preface

The civilization familiar to most readers of this book is considered "post-Christian" though in practice it is often quite anti-Christian. Therefore, it is of the greatest value to let the noble words, deeds and heroic deaths of these forgotten martyrs shine forth again like a brilliant beacon, thereby removing the bushel-basket of obscurity that the post-Christian world endeavors to throw over them.

To begin, let us look at why the concept of martyrdom was so critical to the spread of Christianity, and how, from the very beginning, offering one's life for the Gospel was a paradigm set down by our Blessed Lord Himself as an example to be followed.

—Anthony P. Schiavo, Jr.
June 5, 2018

Introduction

> "The Lord Jesus not only gave His martyrs their instructions, He also strengthened them by His example. I mean, that they might have something to follow when they were about to suffer, He first suffered for them. He pointed out the journey to be made; He made the road along which to make it."
>
> —**Saint Augustine**, Sermon 273,
> *On the birthday of the Martyrs Fructuosus, Bishop, and Augurius and Eulogius, Deacons*[1]

During His public preaching, Jesus predicted that His Church would be a Church of martyrs. Here are a few examples of Our Lord's own words in the Gospels foretelling the tribulations that his followers would endure and how they should act when put to persecution:

> "The brother also shall deliver up the brother to death, and the father the son: and the children shall rise up against their parents, and shall put them to death. And you shall be hated by all men for my name's sake. But he that shall persevere unto the end, he shall be saved. And when they shall persecute you in this city, flee into another."[2]

> "And you shall hear of wars and rumors of wars. See that ye be not troubled. For these things must come to pass, but the end is not yet. For nation shall rise against nation, and kingdom

against kingdom, and there shall be pestilences, and famines, and earthquakes in places. Now all these are the beginnings of sorrows. Then shall they deliver you up to be afflicted, and shall put you to death, and you shall be hated by all nations for my name's sake. And then shall many be scandalized, and shall betray one another, and shall hate one another."[3]

"These things have I spoken to you, that you may not be scandalized. They will put you out of the synagogues: yea, the hour cometh, that whosoever killeth you, will think that he doth a service to God. And these things will they do to you; because they have not known the Father, nor me."[4]

Though He often leveled the accusation of hypocrisy against His opponents, none could name Our Lord a hypocrite. What He called His disciples to endure, He Himself endured without complaint to the highest degree. Jesus of Nazareth experienced a humiliating and horribly painful death, being scourged, beaten, and tortured. After having suffered to the point of complete physical exhaustion, he was forced to carry a heavy cross to the place of his execution. He was then affixed to the timbers, hanging there three hours by the nails which pierced his hands and feet before finally dying. The suffering and death of Jesus are related with compelling witness in the four authentic Gospels of Saints Matthew, Mark, Luke, and John.

The trial, torture and death of Jesus would serve as a prototype to emulate for His Apostles and disciples, as well as for the next two-and-a-half centuries of Christian martyrs.

NOTES

1. This quote is taken from *The Works of Saint Augustine, Sermons III/8 (273-305A) On the Saints* as translated by Edmund Hill, page 17. See Chapter 13 of the present volume for an account of the martyrdom of Saint Fructuosus.
2. Matthew 10:21-23. All passages from Sacred Scripture quoted in this book are taken from the Douay-Rheims-Challoner English translation. These may be conveniently accessed at: http://www.drbo.org.
3. Matthew 24:6-10.
4. John 16:2-3.

The Ancient Sources

Chapter One

The First Martyrs

Where Jesus led, His twelve Apostles faithfully followed. According to long established tradition, all of the Apostles except Saint John the Evangelist were themselves martyred.

The very first martyrdom account is found in Sacred Scripture. The death of Saint Stephen took place shortly after the death and resurrection of Jesus, and is recorded in detail in the Acts of the Apostles. According to the predominance of modern and ancient scholarly opinion, Acts was written by the evangelist Saint Luke around the year AD 65. Luke's description of the death of Stephen is offered below:

The Martyrdom Account of Saint Stephen

> And in those days, the number of the disciples increasing, there arose a murmuring of the Greeks against the Hebrews, for that their widows were neglected in the daily ministration. Then the twelve calling together the multitude of the disciples, said: "It is not reason that we should leave the word of God, and serve tables. Wherefore, brethren, look ye out among you seven men of good reputation, full of the Holy Ghost and wisdom, whom we may appoint over this business. But we will give ourselves continually to prayer, and to the ministry of the word."
>
> And the saying was liked by all the multitude. And they chose Stephen, a man full of faith and of the Holy Ghost, and Philip, and Prochorus, and Nicanor, and Timon, and Parmenas,

and Nicolas, a proselyte of Antioch.

These they set before the apostles, and they praying, imposed hands upon them. And the word of the Lord increased, and the number of the disciples was multiplied in Jerusalem exceedingly: a great multitude also of the priests obeyed the faith. And Stephen, full of grace and fortitude, did great wonders and signs among the people.

Now there arose some of that which is called the synagogue of the Libertines, and of the Cyrenians, and of the Alexandrians, and of them that were of Cilicia and Asia, disputing with Stephen. And they were not able to resist the wisdom and the spirit that spoke. Then they suborned men to say, they had heard him speak words of blasphemy against Moses and against God. And they stirred up the people, and the ancients, and the scribes, and running together, they took him, and brought him to the council. And they set up false witnesses, who said: "This man ceaseth not to speak words against the holy place and the law. For we have heard him say, that this Jesus of Nazareth shall destroy this place, and shall change the traditions which Moses delivered unto us."

And all that sat in the council, looking on him, saw his face as if it had been the face of an angel.

Then the high priest said: "Are these things so?"

Who said: "Ye men, brethren, and fathers, hear....

Here, Stephen gives an extended lecture on salvation history from the time of Abraham and Moses to the time of the prophets. See Acts 7:2–50 for the complete teaching. He concludes:

"You stiffnecked and uncircumcised in heart and ears, you always resist the Holy Ghost. As your fathers did, so do you also. Which of the prophets have not your fathers persecuted? And they have slain them who foretold of the coming of the Just One. Of whom you have been now the betrayers and murderers: Who have received the law by the disposition of angels, and have not kept it."

Now hearing these things, they were cut to the heart, and they gnashed with their teeth at him.

But he, being full of the Holy Ghost, looking up steadfastly to heaven, saw the glory of God, and Jesus standing on the right hand of God. And he said: "Behold, I see the heavens opened, and the Son of man standing on the right hand of God."

And they crying out with a loud voice, stopped their ears, and with one accord ran violently upon him. And casting him forth without the city, they stoned him, and the witnesses laid down their garments at the feet of a young man, whose name was Saul. And they stoned Stephen, invoking and saying: "Lord Jesus, receive my spirit." And falling on his knees, he cried with a loud voice, saying: "Lord, lay not this sin to their charge."

And when he had said this, he fell asleep in the Lord.[1]

Saint Stephen would be the first in a long line of martyrs who died for the sake of the Gospel of Jesus Christ.

Following are accounts taken from Sacred Scripture and from early Christian writings which pertain to the persecution and martyrdoms of several of the apostles, particularly Saints Peter, Paul, James the Greater and James the Less.

Martyrdom of Saints Peter and Paul

The Gospel of Saint John was set down about AD 95. In it, the evangelist records the words of Jesus speaking to Saint Peter, predicting his martyrdom:

> "Amen, amen I say to thee, when thou wast younger, thou didst gird thyself, and didst walk where thou wouldst. But when thou shalt be old, thou shalt stretch forth thy hands, and another shall gird thee, and lead thee whither thou wouldst not.' And this He said, signifying by what death he should glorify God."[2]

Meanwhile, in his second letter to the Corinthians, Saint Paul describes the various persecutions he endured:

They are the ministers of Christ (I speak as one less wise). I am more: in many more labors, in prisons more frequently, in stripes above measure, in deaths often. Of the Jews five times did I receive forty stripes, save one. Thrice was I beaten with rods, once I was stoned, thrice I suffered shipwreck, a night and a day I was in the depth of the sea.[3]

Later, Paul writes to Timothy and foretells his own death. This letter was probably written while Paul was in prison in Rome:

For I am even now ready to be sacrificed and the time of my dissolution is at hand. I have fought a good fight, I have finished my course, I have kept the faith.[4]

Saints Peter and Paul were both martyred in Rome during the reign of Nero, about AD 65. Though no accounts of their martyrdoms survive from the 1st century AD, numerous mentions of the place and method of their executions survive in a variety of later ancient sources, giving the impression that these facts were part of a common wisdom among early Christians.

Here are two notices about the martyrdoms of Peter and Paul. The first is drawn from Origen, a Christian teacher who was active in the early 3rd century AD, as recorded by the first true historian of the ancient Church, Eusebius Pamphilus.

Peter appears to have preached in Pontus, Galatia, Bithynia, Cappadocia, and Asia to the Jews of the dispersion. And at last, having come to Rome, he was crucified head-downwards, for he had requested that he might suffer in this way. What do we need to say concerning Paul, who preached the Gospel of Christ from Jerusalem to Illyricum, and afterwards suffered martyrdom in Rome under Nero? These facts are related by Origen in the third volume of his Commentary on Genesis.[5]

The second passage is from Tertullian, the great Christian apologist of Roman Africa, and is also dated from the early 3rd century AD:

Come now, thou who wish to exercise thy curiosity to better purpose in the business of thy salvation. Go through the Apostolic Churches where the very thrones of the Apostles at this very day preside over their own districts, where their own genuine letters are read which speak their words and bring the presence of each before our minds.

"If Achaia [Greece] is nearest to thee, thou hast Corinth. If thou art not far from Macedonia, thou hast Philippi. If thou canst travel into Asia, thou hast Ephesus. Or if thou art near to Italy, thou hast Rome, where we too have an authority close at hand. What a happy Church is that whereon the Apostles poured out their whole doctrine together with their blood, where Peter suffers a passion like his Lord's, where Paul is crowned with the death of John [the Baptist], whence John the Apostle, after being immersed in boiling oil and taking no hurt, is banished to an island.[6]

As a final ancient testimony, there is a poem of Prudentius taken from his work entitled Peristephanon, *or* The Martyr's Garland. *Written in the late 4th century AD, the poem reflects what a pilgrim of that time might have experienced when visiting the shrines of the holy martyrs Peter and Paul in Rome during their feast days, and in the process offers some details of their martyrdoms. More poems from the* Peristephanon *may be found in Chapters 18 and 19 of the present volume.*

Prudentius on the Martyrdom of Saint Peter and Saint Paul

> May, friend, what means this stir today? What summons gathers all
>   These happy troops along the streets of Rome?
> The feast ennobled by the blood of Peter and of Paul
>   Calls forth the worshippers to leave their home.
>
> The self-same day with interval of one revolving year
>   Beheld the pair by death triumphant crowned.
> Full well doth Father Tiber know, gliding those marshes near,
>   Hallowed with trophies twain that turfy ground.

I AM A CHRISTIAN

Both Cross and Sword he witnessed, twice the ghastly shower saw fall,
   The self-same herb bedewed with martyr's blood.
A victim first fell Peter, in Nero's judgment-hall
   Condemned to hang upon the towering wood.

But he, in fear to emulate his Master, cannot brook
   To court the doom that our salvation earned:
And he claimeth from his murderer one boon, that he may look
   On the Tree's nether limb with head down-turned.

So then his hands transfixed below, the top his feet upbore:
   Greater in spirit as more vile in guise,
Remembering "Who abaseth self exalted shall he soar,"
   To give his soul to heaven, he bowed his eyes.

Soon as the circling seasons brought the swift recurring date,
   And Orient Sun reushered in the day,
The tyrant spat on holy Paul the venom of his hate,
   Christ's world-worn Teacher resolute to slay.

He had seen the goal—had written "I am ready to depart
   And be with Christ," with heaven-inspired pen.
The headsman does his office. Beats no more that noble heart;
   Nor day nor hour has failed his prescient ken.

On either bank, nigh each to each, their ashes now repose,
   Where winds the stream between the two hallowed graves;
The gilded shrine that on the right doth Peter's bones enclose
   'Neath sough of olives sacred Tiber laves.

Trickling adown the slope from brow of overhanging hill,
   There oozes a perennial source of oil.
That fountain flows through fabric now of costly marble, till
   In gleaming bath its circling eddies boil.

Below with hollow undertone the rushing streams descend
   From sparkling basin, white as drifted snow;
Art's many-colored hues above with amber wavelets blend
   Resplendent moss and gold's green-tinted glow.

Lo! where with mantling purple overshadowed lies the pool,
  The fretted roof reflected seems to swim.
Christ the true Shepherd there portrayed, to waters clean and cool,
  Is leading on His flock that thirst for Him.

By Tiber's current, where the turf on the left bank is grazed,
  And Ostia's road guardeth the hallowed ground,
Our prince's favor there to Paul a stately fane upraised,
  And pranked with golden plates the circuit round.

With branching foil of metal blaze on high the burnished beams,
  The aisles are ruddy as the morning ray;
Of pillars white 'neath gilded vault a fourfold order gleams,
  And arches dyed as green as leas in May.

The Father gave these pledges to the nation of the gown:
  To be revered for aye twin temples spring;
Two roads lead forth Rome's worshippers, to feasts one light doth crown,
  To each we hasten, and at each we sing.

Where Tiber's spanned by Hadrian's bridge, we reach the stream's left side:
  From vigil and from ritual the priest
Thither hies back to offerings fresh. Thus Rome keeps holy tide:
  Now homeward wend and celebrate each feast.[7]

Martyrdom of Saint James the Greater

Saint James the Greater was the son of Zebedee and the brother of Saint John the Evangelist. It was he who, along with his brother, Our Lord would nickname, "The Sons of Thunder." The death of James is foretold by Jesus, who says the following in the Gospel according to Matthew:

Then came to Him the mother of the sons of Zebedee with her sons, adoring and asking something of Him. Who said to her, "What wilt thou?"

She saith to Him: "Say that these my two sons may sit, the one on thy right hand, and the other on thy left, in thy kingdom."

And Jesus answering, said: "You know not what you ask. Can you drink the chalice that I shall drink?"

They say to Him: "We can."

He saith to them: "My chalice indeed you shall drink, but to sit on my right or left hand, is not mine to give to you, but to them for whom it is prepared by my Father."[8]

James the Greater is the only Apostle whose death is recorded in Sacred Scripture and took place around AD 44:

And at the same time, Herod the king stretched forth his hands, to afflict some of the church. And he killed James, the brother of John, with the sword.[9]

Writing in the late 2nd or early 3rd century, Saint Clement of Alexandria records an additional anecdote about the death of Saint James the Greater which has come down to us via Eusebius:

And of this James, Clement also relates an anecdote worthy of remembrance in the seventh book of the *Hypotyposes*, from a tradition of his predecessors. He says that the man who brought him to trial, on seeing him bear his testimony, was moved, and confessed that he was a Christian himself. Accordingly, he says, they were both led away together, and on the way the other asked James to forgive him. And he, considering a little, said, "Peace be to thee," and kissed him. And so both were beheaded together.[10]

Martyrdom of James the Less (James the Just)

James the Less is commonly identified as the son of Clopas and Mary who are mentioned in Sacred Scripture. After the death and resurrection of Jesus, James the Less would go on to become the first bishop of Jerusalem, and the author of the canonical Epistle of Saint James which is found in Sacred Scripture. He is mentioned numerous times in Acts of the Apostles and in the epistles of Saint Paul.

The martyrdom of Saint James the Less is believed to have taken place sometime after AD *65. The following account of his death is drawn from Hegesippus, a Jewish convert to Christianity who was active in the 2nd century* AD. *The works of Hegesippus are largely lost. This fragment was preserved within the* Ecclesiastical History *of Eusebius. In this passage, James is referred to as the "brother of the Lord", which most likely means "cousin" as there is no distinction in the Aramaic language between siblings and cousins. Sacred tradition holds that Clopas was the brother of Saint Joseph, the foster father of Jesus, thus making James the Less a first cousin of Our Lord.*

James, the brother of the Lord, succeeded to the government of the Church in conjunction with the apostles. He has been called the Just by all from the time of our Savior to the present day, for there were many that bore the name of James. He was holy from his mother's womb, and he drank no wine nor strong drink, nor did he eat flesh. No razor came upon his head. He did not anoint himself with oil, and he did not use the bath.

He alone was permitted to enter into the holy place, for he wore not woolen but linen garments. And he was in the habit of entering alone into the temple, and was frequently found upon his knees begging forgiveness for the people, so that his knees became hard like those of a camel, in consequence of his constantly bending them in his worship of God, and asking forgiveness for the people. Because of his exceeding great justice he was called the Just, and *Oblias*, which signifies in Greek 'Bulwark of the people' and 'Justice,' in accordance with what the prophets declare concerning him.

Now some of the seven sects, which existed among the people and which have been mentioned by me in the *Memoirs*, asked him, "What is the gate of Jesus?"

And he replied that He was the Savior. On account of these words some believed that Jesus is the Christ. But the sects mentioned above did not believe either in a resurrection or in one's coming to give to every man according to his works. But as many as believed did so on account of James. Therefore when many even of the rulers believed, there was a commotion among the Jews and Scribes and Pharisees, who said that there was danger that the whole people would be looking for Jesus as the Christ.

Coming therefore in a body to James they said, "We entreat thee, restrain the people, for they are gone astray in regard to Jesus, as if he were the Christ. We entreat thee to persuade all that have come to the feast of the Passover concerning Jesus, for we all have confidence in thee. For we bear thee witness, as do all the people, that thou art just, and dost not respect persons. Do thou therefore persuade the multitude not to be led astray concerning Jesus. For the whole people, and all of us also, have confidence in thee. Stand therefore upon the pinnacle of the temple, that from that high position thou mayest be clearly seen, and that thy words may be readily heard by all the people. For all the tribes, with the Gentiles also, are come together on account of the Passover."

The aforesaid Scribes and Pharisees therefore placed James upon the pinnacle of the temple, and cried out to him and said: "Thou just one, in whom we ought all to have confidence, forasmuch as the people are led astray after Jesus, the crucified one, declare to us, what is the gate of Jesus."

And he answered with a loud voice, "Why do ye ask me concerning Jesus, the Son of Man? He himself sitteth in heaven at the right hand of the great Power, and is about to come upon the clouds of heaven."

And when many were fully convinced and gloried in the testimony of James, and said, "Hosanna to the Son of David," these same Scribes and Pharisees said again to one another, "We have done badly in supplying such testimony to Jesus. But let us go up and throw him down, in order that they may be afraid to believe him."

And they cried out, saying, "Oh! oh! the just man is also in error." And they fulfilled the Scripture written in Isaiah, "Let us take away the just man, because he is troublesome to us: therefore they shall eat the fruit of their doings."[11]

So they went up and threw down the just man, and said

to each other, "Let us stone James the Just." And they began to stone him, for he was not killed by the fall.

But he turned and knelt down and said, "I entreat thee, Lord God our Father, forgive them, for they know not what they do."

And while they were thus stoning him one of the priests of the sons of Rechab, the son of the Rechabites, who are mentioned by Jeremiah the prophet, cried out, saying, "Cease, what do ye? The just one prayeth for you."

And one of them, who was a fuller, took the club with which he beat out clothes and struck the just man on the head. And thus he suffered martyrdom. And they buried him on the spot, by the temple, and his monument still remains by the temple. He became a true witness, both to Jews and Greeks, that Jesus is the Christ. And immediately Vespasian besieged them."[12]

As a transition between the martyrdom accounts of the Apostles and those of the early Christian saints in subsequent chapters, we offer the following excerpt from the Epistle of Mathetes to Diognetus, *an early Christian apologetical work dating perhaps from the mid-2nd century* AD. *In this work, the unknown author named Mathetes (which in Greek means, simply, a disciple) explains the various aspects of Christian doctrine, morals and philosophy to a learned pagan named Diognetus.*

The excerpt below offers an excellent window into how the early Christians perceived themselves and their situation among the pagan population of the Roman Empire. The last paragraph is particularly instructive as to how the early Christians viewed the persecutions they endured.

THE MANNERS OF THE CHRISTIANS

For the Christians are distinguished from other men neither by country, nor language, nor the customs which they observe. For they neither inhabit cities of their own, nor employ a peculiar form of speech, nor lead a life which is marked out by any singularity.

The course of conduct which they follow has not been devised by any speculation or deliberation of inquisitive men. Nor do they, like some, proclaim themselves the advocates of any merely human doctrines. But, inhabiting Greek as well as barbarian cities, according as the lot of each of them has determined, and following the customs of the natives in respect to clothing, food, and the rest of their ordinary conduct, they display to us their wonderful and confessedly striking method of life.

They dwell in their own countries, but simply as sojourners. As citizens, they share in all things with others, and yet endure all things as if foreigners. Every foreign land is to them as their native country, and every land of their birth as a land of strangers. They marry, as do all [others]. They beget children, but they do not destroy their offspring. They have a common table, but not a common bed. They are in the flesh, but they do not live after the flesh. They pass their days on earth, but they are citizens of heaven.

They obey the prescribed laws, and at the same time surpass the laws by their lives. They love all men, and are persecuted by all. They are unknown and condemned. They are put to death, and restored to life. They are poor, yet make many rich. They are in lack of all things, and yet abound in all. They are dishonored, and yet in their very dishonor are glorified. They are evil spoken of, and yet are justified. They are reviled, and bless. They are insulted, and repay the insult with honor. They do good, yet are punished as evil-doers. When punished, they rejoice as if quickened into life. They are assailed by the Jews as foreigners, and are persecuted by the Greeks, yet those who hate them are unable to assign any reason for their hatred.[13]

Throughout the 1st century AD, *persecution of the early Christians was sporadic and incidental, usually occurring due to charges that their preaching the Gospel stirred up the people and caused unrest. As is well known from the Passion accounts of Jesus, Roman governors tended to*

have little sympathy for perceived rabble-rousers. General outbreaks of violence against Christian communities remained, however, quite rare.

One such eruption was the persecution in Rome spurred on by the Roman emperor Nero in the early 60s AD. The pagan Roman historian, Tacitus, writing about 50 years after the events, records that after the great fire of Rome, gossip emerged that Nero had started the fire himself. Tacitus relates that "to scotch the rumor, Nero substituted as culprits and punished with the utmost refinements of cruelty, a class of men loathed for their vices whom the crowd styled Christians."

Further in the same passage, Tacitus describes how the persecution progressed:

> The confessed members of the sect were arrested. Next on their disclosures, vast numbers were convicted, not so much on the count of arson as for hatred of the human race. And derision accompanied their end: they were covered with wild beasts' skins and torn to death by dogs, or they were fastened on crosses and, when daylight failed were burned to serve as lamps by night. Nero had offered his Gardens for the spectacle, and gave an exhibition in his Circus, mixing with the crowd in the habit of a charioteer, or mounted on his car. Hence, in spite of a guilt which had earned the most exemplary punishment, there arose a sentiment of pity, due to the impression that they were being sacrificed not for the welfare of the state but to the ferocity of a single man.[14]

Following Nero's death, hostility toward the Christians seemed to cool. The Church experienced a period of peace and growth for a few decades as the empire grappled with numerous political issues and wars both internal and foreign. The peace, however, would not last.

NOTES

1. Acts of the Apostles 6:1-15, 7:1, and 7:50-59.
2. John 21:18-19.
3. 2 Corinthians 11:23-25.
4. 2 Timothy 4:6-7.
5. This passage from Origen was recorded by Eusebius Pamphilius in his *Ecclesiastical*

History, Book III, Chapter 1, and was taken from *A Select Library of Nicene and Post-Nicene Fathers of the Christian Church, Volume I: Eusebius*, translated by Arthur C. McGiffert. See the Sources section at the end of this book for a complete listing of the ancient and modern works referred to in this book.
6. This treatise of Tertullian may be found in *On the Testimony of the Soul and On the Prescription of Heretics*, translated by T. Herbert Bindley.
7. Many of the poems of Prudentius from the *Peristephanon*—including this one—may be found translated into English by Francis St. John Thackeray in *Translations from Prudentius*.
8. Matthew 20:20-23.
9. Acts of the Apostles 12:1-2.
10. This excerpt from Clement of Alexandria was preserved in the *Ecclesiastical History* of Eusebius Pamphilus, Book II, Chapter 9.
11. This is a rendering of Isaiah 3:10 from the Greek Septuagint.
12. This account of Hegesippus was preserved by Eusebius Pamphilus in his Ecclesiastical History, Book II, Chapter 23.
13. An English version of *The Letter to Diognetus* may be found in *Ante-Nicene Fathers, Volume 1: The Apostolic Fathers*, translated by Alexander Roberts and James Donaldson.
14. This excerpt from Tacitus is taken from *Annals*, Book 15, Chapter 44, as translated by John Jackson.

Chapter 2

The Passion of Saint Ignatius of Antioch

The next instance of state-sponsored persecution of Christians seemed to erupt during the reign of the emperor Domitian (AD 81–96). In contrast to the brutal executions under Nero, however, the magistrates under Domitian generally did not execute Christians, but rather sentenced them to exile. Saint John the Evangelist, exiled to the island of Patmos, and Domitian's niece, Flavia Domitilla, exiled to the island of Pandateria, were examples of the latter. Known martyrs from this period are few. Men like Clemens and Glabrio who were executed for "atheism" may have been Christians, but their status remains very much in doubt. See the Epitaph of Achilleus and Nereus in the Appendix of this book for more information about Domitilla, Clemens and Glabrio.

With the assassination of Domitian and the advent of the so-called "Five Good Emperors", the legal status of Christians was clarified, though perhaps not for the better. There exists a noteworthy correspondence between the emperor Trajan who reigned from AD 90 through 117, and Pliny the Younger, written while the latter was serving as a legate in Bithynia. Pliny asked the emperor for advice on how to deal with Christians who had been denounced to him. Trajan's famous reply has survived antiquity:

> You have followed the right procedure, my dear Pliny, in investigating the cases of those who had been brought before

you as Christians. For, indeed, it is not possible to establish any universal rule possessing, as it were, a fixed form. These people should not be searched for. If they are denounced and convicted, they should be punished. Yet, if any one shall deny being a Christian, and shall make this plain in action, that is, by worshipping our gods, even though suspected on account of his past conduct, he shall obtain pardon by his penitence.

Anonymous denunciations, however, ought not to be allowed standing in any kind of charge, as this is a course which would not only form the worst of precedents, but it is not in accordance with the spirit of our time."¹

This model of dealing with Christians would be followed with greater or lesser intensity by the magistrates of the Roman state for the next century.

Saint Ignatius of Antioch belonged to the generation immediately after the passing of the Apostles. He was condemned in Antioch, though his martyrdom took place in Rome, and occurred sometime during the reign of the emperor Trajan. The authenticity of this passion has been accepted by the majority of scholars down through the ages, though the identity of the accuser—whether it be Trajan himself or one of his magistrates—may be called into question. We know that Trajan visited Antioch thanks to a notice in the History *of Cassius Dio which mentions that the emperor visited the city in preparation for his campaign against the Parthians and was present there during the devastating earthquake of* AD *115.*²

As the introductory sentences to this passion make clear, Ignatius was a disciple of Saint John the Evangelist. There is an ancient legend that says that he acquired the name "Theophorus" because he was in fact the child mentioned in the Gospel of Matthew 18:2 who was placed before the Apostles by Our Lord as a model of simplicity. It is likely that this account of his passion and death was written by his companions mentioned in another of his works namely, Philo, Agathopus and Crocus.

The Martyrdom of Ignatius of Antioch

Chapter I. Desire of Ignatius for Martyrdom.

When Trajan, not long since, succeeded to the empire of the Romans, Ignatius, the disciple of John the Apostle, a man in all respects of an apostolic character, governed the Church of the Antiochians with great care, having with difficulty escaped the former storms of the many persecutions under Domitian. Like a good pilot, by the helm of prayer and fasting, by the earnestness of his teaching, and by his [constant] spiritual labor, he resisted the flood that rolled against him, fearing [only] lest he should lose any of those who were deficient in courage, or apt to suffer from their simplicity.

Wherefore he rejoiced over the tranquil state of the Church when the persecution ceased for a little time, but was grieved as to himself, that he had not yet attained to a true love to Christ, nor reached the perfect rank of a disciple. For he inwardly reflected that the confession which is made by martyrdom would bring him into a yet more intimate relation to the Lord. Wherefore, continuing a few years longer with the Church and, like a divine lamp, enlightening every one's understanding by his expositions of the [Holy] Scriptures, he [at length] attained the object of his desire.

Chapter II. Ignatius is Condemned by Trajan.

For Trajan, in the ninth year of his reign, being lifted up [with pride] after the victory he had gained over the Scythians and Dacians and many other nations, and thinking that the religious body of the Christians were yet wanting to complete the subjugation of all things to himself, and [thereupon] threatening them with persecution unless they should agree to worship dæmons, as did all other nations, thus compelled all who were living godly lives either to sacrifice [to idols] or die. Wherefore the noble soldier of Christ [Ignatius], being in fear for the Church of the Antiochians was, in accordance with his own desire, brought before Trajan, who was at that time staying at Antioch, but was in haste [to set forth] against Armenia and the Parthians.

And when he was set before the emperor Trajan, [that prince] said unto him, "Who art thou, wicked wretch, who settest thyself to transgress our commands, and persuadest others to do the same, so that they should miserably perish?"

Ignatius replied, "No one ought to call Theophorus wicked, for all evil spirits have departed from the servants of God. But if because I am an enemy to these [spirits], you call me wicked in respect to them, I quite agree with you. For inasmuch as I have Christ the King of heaven [within me], I destroy all the devices of these [evil spirits]."

Trajan answered, "And who is Theophorus?"

Ignatius replied, "He who has Christ within his breast."

Trajan said, "Do *we* not then seem to you to have the gods in our mind, whose assistance we enjoy in fighting against our enemies?"

Ignatius answered, "Thou art in error when thou callest the dæmons of the nations gods. For there is but one God, who made heaven, and earth, and the sea, and all that are in them. And one Jesus Christ, the only-begotten Son of God, whose kingdom may I enjoy."

Trajan said, "Do you mean Him who was crucified under Pontius Pilate?"

Ignatius replied, "I mean Him who crucified my sin, with him who was the inventor of it, and who has condemned [and cast down] all the deceit and malice of the devil under the feet of those who carry Him in their heart."

Trajan said, "Dost thou then carry within thee Him that was crucified?"

Ignatius replied, "Truly so, for it is written, 'I will dwell in them, and walk in them.'"[3]

Then Trajan pronounced sentence as follows: "We command that Ignatius, who affirms that he carries about within him Him that was crucified, be bound by soldiers, and carried to the great [city] Rome, there to be devoured by the beasts, for the gratification of the people."

When the holy martyr heard this sentence, he cried out with joy, "I thank thee, O Lord, that Thou hast vouchsafed to honor me with a perfect love towards Thee, and hast made me to be bound with iron chains, like Thy Apostle Paul."

Having spoken thus, he then with delight clasped the chains about him, and when he had first prayed for the Church, and commended it with tears to the Lord, he was hurried away by the savage cruelty of the soldiers like a distinguished ram the leader of a goodly flock, that he might be carried to Rome, there to furnish food to the bloodthirsty beasts.

Chapter III. Ignatius Sails to Smyrna.

Wherefore, with great alacrity and joy through his desire to suffer, he came down from Antioch to Seleucia from which place he set sail. And after a great deal of suffering he came to Smyrna, where he disembarked with great joy and hastened to see the holy Polycarp, [formerly] his fellow-disciple and [now] bishop of Smyrna. For they had both, in old times, been disciples of Saint John the Apostle. Being then brought to him and having communicated to him some spiritual gifts and glorying in his bonds, he entreated of him to labor along with him for the fulfillment of his desire, earnestly indeed asking this of the whole Church (for the cities and Churches of Asia had welcomed the holy man through their bishops, and presbyters, and deacons, all hastening to meet him if by any means they might receive from him some spiritual gift), but above all, the holy Polycarp that by means of the wild beasts he soon disappearing from this world, might be manifested before the face of Christ.

Chapter IV. Ignatius Writes to the Churches.

And these things he thus spake and thus testified, extending his love to Christ so far as one who was about to secure heaven through his good confession and the earnestness of those who joined their prayers to his in regard to his [approaching] conflict, and to give a recompense to the Churches, who came to meet him through their rulers, sending letters of thanksgiving to them, which dropped spiritual grace along with prayer and exhortation. Wherefore, seeing all men so kindly affected towards him and fearing lest the love of the brotherhood should hinder his zeal towards the Lord while a fair door of suffering martyrdom was opened to him, he wrote to the Church of the Romans the Epistle which is here subjoined.[4]

Chapter V. Ignatius is Brought to Rome.

Having therefore by means of this Epistle settled, as he wished, those of the brethren at Rome who were unwilling [for his martyrdom], and setting sail from Smyrna (for Christophorus was pressed by the soldiers to hasten to the public spectacles in the mighty [city] Rome that, being given up to the wild beasts in the sight of the Roman people, he might attain to the crown for which he strove), he [next] landed at Troas. Then, going on from that place to Neapolis, he went [on foot] by Philippi through Macedonia, and on to that part of Epirus which is near Epidamnus. And finding a ship in one of the seaports, he sailed over the Adriatic Sea, and entering from it on the Tyrrhene, he passed by the various islands and cities until, when Puteoli came in sight, he was eager there to disembark, having a desire to tread in the footsteps of the Apostle Paul. But a violent wind arising did not suffer him to do so, the ship being driven rapidly forwards, and simply expressing his delight over the love of the brethren in that place, he sailed by.

Wherefore, continuing to enjoy fair winds, we were reluctantly hurried on in one day and a night, mourning [as we did] over the coming departure from us of this righteous man. But to him this happened just as he wished, since he was in haste as soon as possible to leave this world that he might attain to the Lord whom he loved. Sailing then into the Roman harbor, and the unhallowed sports being just about to close, the soldiers began to be annoyed at our slowness, but the bishop rejoicingly yielded to their urgency.

Chapter VI. Ignatius is Devoured by the Beasts at Rome.

They pushed forth therefore from the place which is called Portus, and (the fame of all relating to the holy martyr being already spread abroad) we met the brethren full of fear and joy, rejoicing indeed because they were thought worthy to meet with Theophorus but struck with fear because so eminent a man was being led to death. Now he enjoined some to keep silence who in their fervent zeal, were saying that they would appease the people so that they should not demand the destruction of this just one. He being immediately aware of this through the Spirit and having saluted them all and begged of them to show a true affection towards him, and having dwelt [on this point] at greater length than in his Epistle, and having persuaded them not to envy him hastening to the Lord, he then, after he had with all the brethren kneeling [beside him] entreated the Son of God in behalf of the Churches that a stop might be put to the persecution and that mutual love might continue among the brethren, was led with all haste into the amphitheater.

Then, being immediately thrown in according to the command of Cæsar given some time ago, the public spectacles being just about to close (for it was then a solemn day, as they deemed it, being that which is called the thirteenth in the Roman tongue, on which the people were wont to assemble in more than ordinary numbers), he was thus cast to the wild beasts close beside the temple that so by them the desire of the holy martyr Ignatius should be fulfilled according to that which is written, "The desire of the righteous is acceptable [to God],"[5] to the effect that he might not be troublesome to any of the brethren by the gathering of his remains, even as he had in his Epistle expressed a wish beforehand that so his end might be. For only the harder portions of his holy remains were left, which were conveyed to Antioch and wrapped in linen as an inestimable treasure left to the holy Church by the grace which was in the martyr.

I AM A CHRISTIAN

Chapter VII. Ignatius Appears in a Vision After His Death.

Now these things took place on the thirteenth day before the Kalends of January, that is, on the twentieth of December, Sura and Senecio being then the consuls of the Romans for the second time. Having ourselves been eye-witnesses of these things and having spent the whole night in tears within the house and having entreated the Lord with bended knees and much prayer that He would give us weak men full assurance respecting the things which were done, it came to pass on our falling into a brief slumber that some of us saw the blessed Ignatius suddenly standing by us and embracing us, while others beheld him again praying for us, and others still saw him dropping with sweat, as if he had just come from his great labor and standing by the Lord.

When, therefore, we had with great joy witnessed these things and had compared our several visions together, we sang praise to God, the giver of all good things, and expressed our sense of the happiness of the holy [martyr]. And now we have made known to you both the day and the time [when these things happened] that, assembling ourselves together according to the time of his martyrdom, we may have fellowship with the champion and noble martyr of Christ, who trod under foot the devil and perfected the course which, out of love to Christ, he had desired in Christ Jesus our Lord by whom and with whom be glory and power to the Father, with the Holy Spirit, for evermore! Amen.[6]

NOTES

1. Pliny's original letter and the response from Trajan reproduced here may be found in *The Letters of the Younger Pliny* 97 (98) as translated by John Delaware Lewis.
2. Taken from the *History* of Cassius Dio, Book LXVIII, Chapter 24.
3. Leviticus 26:12. Also quoted in 2 Corinthians 6:16.
4. This letter exists to this day. An English translation of the Epistle of Ignatius to the Romans may be found in *The Ante-Nicene Fathers, Volume 1: The Apostolic Fathers*, edited by Alexander Roberts, James Donaldson and A. Cleveland Coxe.
5. This quote probably refers to Proverbs 11:23.
6. This account of the martyrdom of Saint Ignatius of Antioch was taken from *The Ante-Nicene Fathers, Volume I* as mentioned in Note 4 above.

CHAPTER 3

The Passion of Saint Polycarp

In the previous chapter, we read that Ignatius visited his friend and fellow disciple of Saint John, Polycarp, while on his way to his martyrdom in Rome. This Polycarp served as bishop of Smyrna in Asia Minor, and according to Eusebius (quoting Irenæus, one of Polycarp's disciples), he knew many who had met Christ in the flesh. His epistle to the Philippians is extant and he is remembered for his stinging rebuke of the heretic, Marcion who once said upon meeting Polycarp, "Don't you know me?" to which Polycarp replied: "Yes, I know the first-born of Satan."[1]

The account of his martyrdom related below purports to have been written by the church of Smyrna to the church at Philomelium, another city in Asia Minor. Having lived to a very old age, Polycarp served as a bridge from the Apostolic age deep into the second century AD. Eusebius reports that his martyrdom took place during the reign of the emperor Marcus Aurelius, though other sources maintain an earlier date based on evidence that Statius Quadratus, the proconsul mentioned in the martyrdom account, served in Asia in AD 155–156.

THE ENCYCLICAL EPISTLE OF THE CHURCH AT SMYRNA

Concerning the Martyrdom of the Holy Polycarp

The Church of God which sojourns at Smyrna, to the Church of God sojourning in Philomelium, and to all the congregations of the Holy and Catholic Church in every place: Mercy, peace, and love from God the Father, and our Lord Jesus Christ, be multiplied.

Chapter I. Subject of Which We Write.

We have written to you, brethren, as to what relates to the martyrs, and especially to the blessed Polycarp who put an end to the persecution having, as it were, set a seal upon it by his martyrdom. For almost all the events that happened previously [to this one], took place that the Lord might show us from above a martyrdom becoming the Gospel. For he waited to be delivered up, even as the Lord had done, that we also might become his followers, while we look not merely at what concerns ourselves but have regard also to our neighbors. For it is the part of a true and well-founded love, not only to wish one's self to be saved, but also all the brethren.

Chapter II. The Wonderful Constancy of the Martyrs.

All the martyrdoms, then, were blessed and noble which took place according to the will of God. For it becomes us who profess greater piety than others to ascribe the authority over all things to God. And truly, who can fail to admire their nobleness of mind and their patience, with that love towards their Lord which they displayed? Who, when they were so torn with scourges, that the frame of their bodies even to the very inward veins and arteries was laid open, still patiently endured, while even those that stood by pitied and bewailed them. But they reached such a pitch of magnanimity, that not one of them let a sigh or a groan escape them, thus proving to us all that those holy martyrs of Christ, at the very time when they suffered such torments, were absent from the body, or rather, that the Lord then stood by them and communed with them. And, looking to the grace of Christ, they despised all the torments of this world, redeeming themselves from eternal punishment by [the suffering of] a single hour.

For this reason the fire of their savage executioners appeared cool to them. For they kept before their view escape from that fire which is eternal and never shall be quenched and looked forward with the eyes of their heart to those good things which are laid up for such as endure: things "which ear hath not heard, nor eye seen, neither have entered into the heart of man," but were revealed by the Lord to them, inasmuch as they were no longer men but had already become angels. And, in like manner, those who were condemned to the wild beasts endured dreadful tortures, being stretched out upon beds full of spikes and subjected to various other kinds of torments, in order that, if it were possible, the tyrant might, by their lingering tortures, lead them to a denial [of Christ].

Chapter III. The Constancy of Germanicus. The Death of Polycarp is Demanded.

For the devil did indeed invent many things against them, but thanks be to God, he could not prevail over all. For the most noble Germanicus strengthened the timidity of others by his own patience, and fought heroically with the wild beasts. For, when the proconsul sought to persuade him and urged him to take pity upon his age, he attracted the wild beast towards himself and provoked it, being desirous to escape all the more quickly from an unrighteous and impious world. But upon this the whole multitude, marvelling at the nobility of mind displayed by the devout and godly race of Christians, cried out, "Away with the atheists. Let Polycarp be sought out!"

Chapter IV. Quintus the Apostate.

Now one named Quintus, a Phrygian, who was but lately come from Phrygia, when he saw the wild beasts, became afraid. This was the man who forced himself and some others to come forward voluntarily [for trial]. The proconsul, after many entreaties, persuaded him to swear and to offer sacrifice. Wherefore, brethren, we do not commend those who give themselves up [to suffering], seeing the Gospel does not teach so to do.

Chapter V. The Departure and Vision of Polycarp.

But the most admirable Polycarp, when he first heard [that he was sought for], was in no measure disturbed but resolved to continue in the city. However, in deference to the wish of many, he was persuaded to leave it. He departed, therefore, to a country house not far distant from the city. There he stayed with a few [friends] engaged in nothing else night and day than praying for all men and for the Churches throughout the world according to his usual custom. And while he was praying, a vision presented itself to him three days before he was taken, and behold, the pillow under his head seemed to him on fire. Upon this, turning to those that were with him, he said to them prophetically, "I must be burnt alive."

Chapter VI. Polycarp is Betrayed by a Servant.

And when those who sought for him were at hand, he departed to another dwelling whither his pursuers immediately came after him. And when they found him not, they seized upon two youths [that were there], one of whom, being subjected to torture, confessed. It was thus impossible that he should continue hid, since those that betrayed him were of his own household. The Irenarch then (whose office is the same as that of the Cleronomus), by name Herod, hastened to bring him into the stadium. [This all happened] that he might fulfill his special lot, being made a partaker of Christ, and that they who betrayed him might undergo the punishment of Judas himself.

Chapter VII. Polycarp is Found by His Pursuers.

His pursuers then, along with horsemen and taking the youth with them, went forth at supper-time on the day of the preparation with their usual weapons, as if going out against a robber. And being come about evening [to the place where he was], they found him lying down in the upper room of a certain little house, from which he might have escaped into another place. But he refused, saying, "The will of God be done." So when he heard that they were come, he went down and spoke with them. And as those that were present marvelled at his age and constancy, some of them said. "Was so much effort made to capture such a venerable man?"

Immediately then, in that very hour, he ordered that something to eat and drink should be set before them, as much indeed as they cared for, while he besought them to allow him an hour to pray without disturbance. And on their giving him leave, he stood and prayed, being full of the grace of God, so that he could not cease for two full hours, to the astonishment of them that heard him, insomuch that many began to repent that they had come forth against so godly and venerable an old man.

Chapter VIII. Polycarp is Brought into the City.

Now as soon as he had ceased praying, having made mention of all that had at any time come in contact with him, both small and great, illustrious and obscure, as well as the whole Catholic Church throughout the world, the time of his departure having arrived, they set him upon an ass and conducted him into the city, the day being that of the great Sabbath. And the Irenarch Herod, accompanied by his father Nicetes (both riding in a chariot) met him, and taking him up into the chariot, they seated themselves beside him and endeavored to persuade him saying, "What harm is there in saying, Lord Cæsar, and in sacrificing, with the other ceremonies observed on such occasions, and so make sure of safety?"

But he at first gave them no answer. And when they continued to urge him, he said, "I shall not do as you advise me."

So they, having no hope of persuading him, began to speak bitter words unto him and cast him with violence out of the chariot, insomuch that in getting down from the carriage, he dislocated his leg [by the fall]. But without being disturbed and as if suffering nothing, he went eagerly forward with all haste and was conducted to the stadium, where the tumult was so great that there was no possibility of being heard.

Chapter IX. Polycarp Refuses to Revile Christ.

Now, as Polycarp was entering into the stadium, there came to him a voice from heaven, saying, "Be strong, and show thyself a man, O Polycarp!" No one saw who it was that spoke to him, but those of our brethren who were present heard the voice.

As he was brought forward, the tumult became great when they heard that Polycarp was taken. And when he came near, the proconsul asked him whether he was Polycarp. On his confessing that he was, [the proconsul] sought to persuade him to deny [Christ] saying, "Have respect to thy old age," and other similar things, according to their custom, [such as], "Swear by the fortune of Cæsar. Repent and say, 'Away with the atheists.'"

But Polycarp, gazing with a stern countenance on all the multitude of the wicked heathen then in the stadium and waving his hand towards them, while with groans he looked up to heaven said, "Away with the atheists."

Then, the proconsul urging him and saying, "Swear, and I will set thee at liberty, reproach Christ."

Polycarp declared, "Eighty-and-six years have I served Him, and He never did me any injury. How then can I blaspheme my King and my Savior?"

Chapter X. Polycarp Confesses Himself a Christian.

And the proconsul yet again pressed him and said, "Swear by the fortune of Cæsar."

He answered, "Since thou art vainly urgent that, as thou sayest, I should swear by the fortune of Cæsar and pretendest not to know who and what I am, hear me declare with boldness: I am a Christian. And if you wish to learn what the doctrines of Christianity are, appoint me a day and thou shalt hear them."

The proconsul replied, "Persuade the people."

But Polycarp said, "To thee I have thought it right to offer an account [of my faith], for we are taught to give all due honor (which entails no injury upon ourselves) to the powers and authorities which are ordained of God. But as for these, I do not deem them worthy of receiving any account from me."

Chapter XI. No Threats Have Any Effect on Polycarp.

The proconsul then said to him, "I have wild beasts at hand. To these will I cast thee, except thou repent."

But he answered, "Call them then, for we are not accustomed to repent of what is good in order to adopt that which is evil, and it is well for me to be changed from what is evil to what is righteous."

But again the proconsul said to him, "I will cause thee to be consumed by fire, seeing thou despisest the wild beasts, if thou wilt not repent."

But Polycarp said, "Thou threatenest me with fire which burneth for an hour and after a little is extinguished, but art ignorant of the fire of the coming judgment and of eternal punishment reserved for the ungodly. But why tarriest thou? Bring forth what thou wilt."

Chapter XII. Polycarp is Sentenced to Be Burned.

While he spoke these and many other like things, he was filled with confidence and joy and his countenance was full of grace, so that not merely did it not fall as if troubled by the things said to him, but on the contrary, the proconsul was astonished and sent his herald to proclaim in the midst of the stadium thrice, "Polycarp has confessed that he is a Christian."

This proclamation having been made by the herald, the whole multitude both of the heathen and Jews who dwelt at Smyrna cried out with uncontrollable fury and in a loud voice, "This is the teacher of Asia, the father of the Christians, and the overthrower of our gods, he who has been teaching many not to sacrifice or to worship the gods." Speaking thus, they cried out and besought Philip the Asiarch to let loose a lion upon Polycarp. But Philip answered that it was not lawful for him to do so, seeing the shows of wild beasts were already finished.

Then it seemed good to them to cry out with one consent that Polycarp should be burnt alive. For thus it behooved the vision which was revealed to him in regard to his pillow to be fulfilled when, seeing it on fire as he was praying, he turned about and said prophetically to the faithful that were with him, "I must be burnt alive."

Chapter XIII. The Funeral Pile is Erected.

This, then, was carried into effect with greater speed than it was spoken, the multitudes immediately gathering together wood and fagots out of the shops and baths, the Jews especially according to custom eagerly assisting them in it. And when the funeral pile was ready, Polycarp, laying aside all his garments, and loosing his girdle, sought also to take off his sandals—a thing he was not accustomed to do inasmuch as every one of the faithful was always eager who should first touch his skin. For on account of his holy life he was, even before his martyrdom, adorned with every kind of good. Immediately then they surrounded him with those substances which had been prepared for the funeral pile. But when they were about also to fix him with nails, he said, "Leave me as I am. For He that giveth me strength to endure the fire, will also enable me, without your securing me by nails, to remain without moving in the pile."

Chapter XIV. The Prayer of Polycarp.

They did not nail him then, but simply bound him. And he, placing his hands behind him and being bound like a distinguished ram [taken] out of a great flock for sacrifice, and prepared to be an acceptable burnt-offering unto God, looked up to heaven, and said, "O Lord God Almighty, the Father of thy beloved and blessed Son Jesus Christ, by whom we have received the knowledge of Thee, the God of angels and powers, and of every creature, and of the whole race of the righteous who live before thee, I give Thee thanks that Thou hast counted me, worthy of this day and this hour, that I should have a part in the number of Thy martyrs, in the cup of thy Christ, to the resurrection of eternal life, both of soul and body, through the incorruption [imparted] by the Holy Ghost. Among whom may

I be accepted this day before Thee as a fat and acceptable sacrifice, according as Thou, the ever-truthful God, hast foreordained, hast revealed beforehand to me, and now hast fulfilled. Wherefore also I praise Thee for all things, I bless Thee, I glorify Thee, along with the everlasting and heavenly Jesus Christ, Thy beloved Son, with whom to Thee and the Holy Ghost, be glory both now and to all coming ages. Amen."

Chapter XV. Polycarp is Not Injured by the Fire.

When he had pronounced this amen and so finished his prayer, those who were appointed for the purpose kindled the fire. And as the flame blazed forth in great fury we, to whom it was given to witness it, beheld a great miracle and have been preserved that we might report to others what then took place. For the fire, shaping itself into the form of an arch like the sail of a ship when filled with the wind, encompassed as by a circle the body of the martyr. And he appeared within not like flesh which is burnt, but as bread that is baked, or as gold and silver glowing in a furnace. Moreover, we perceived such a sweet odor [coming from the pile], as if frankincense or some such precious spices had been smoking there.

Chapter XVI. Polycarp is Pierced by a Dagger.

At length, when those wicked men perceived that his body could not be consumed by the fire, they commanded an executioner to go near and pierce him through with a dagger. And on his doing this, there came forth a dove and a great quantity of blood, so that the fire was extinguished. And all the people wondered that there should be such a difference between the unbelievers and the elect, of whom this most admirable Polycarp was one, having in our own times been an apostolic and prophetic teacher, and bishop of the Catholic Church which is in Smyrna. For every word that went out of his mouth either has been or shall yet be accomplished.

Chapter XVII. The Christians are Refused Polycarp's Body.

But when the adversary of the race of the righteous, the envious, malicious, and wicked one, perceived the impressive nature of his martyrdom and [considered] the blameless life he had led from the beginning, and how he was now crowned with the wreath of immortality, having beyond dispute received his reward, he did his utmost that not the least memorial of him should be taken away by us, although many desired to do this and to become possessors of his holy flesh. For this end he suggested it to Nicetes, the father of Herod and brother of Alce, to go and entreat the governor not to give up his body to be buried, "lest," said he, "forsaking Him that was crucified, they begin to worship this one."

This he said at the suggestion and urgent persuasion of the Jews, who also watched us as we sought to take him out of the fire, being ignorant of this, that it is neither possible for us ever to forsake Christ who suffered for the salvation of such as shall be saved throughout the whole world (the blameless one for sinners), nor to worship any other. For Him indeed, as being the Son of God, we adore, but the martyrs as disciples and followers of the Lord we worthily love on account of their extraordinary affection towards their own King and Master, of whom may we also be made companions and fellow-disciples!

Chapter XVIII. The Body of Polycarp is Burned.

The centurion then, seeing the strife excited by the Jews, placed the body in the midst of the fire and consumed it. Accordingly, we afterwards took up his bones, as being more precious than the most exquisite jewels and more purified than gold, and deposited them in a fitting place whither being gathered together as opportunity is allowed us with joy and rejoicing, the Lord shall grant us to celebrate the anniversary of his martyrdom, both in memory of those who have already finished their course and for the exercising and preparation of those yet to walk in their steps.

Chapter XIX. Praise of the Martyr Polycarp.

This, then, is the account of the blessed Polycarp who, being the twelfth that was martyred in Smyrna (reckoning those also of Philadelphia), yet occupies a place of his own in the memory of all men insomuch that he is everywhere spoken of by the heathen themselves. He was not merely an illustrious teacher, but also a pre-eminent martyr whose martyrdom all desire to imitate as having been altogether consistent with the Gospel of Christ. For having through patience overcome the unjust governor and thus acquired the crown of immortality, he now with the apostles and all the righteous [in heaven] rejoicingly glorifies God, even the Father, and blesses our Lord Jesus Christ, the Savior of our souls, the Governor of our bodies, and the Shepherd of the Catholic Church throughout the world.

Chapter XX. This Epistle is to Be Transmitted to the Brethren.

Since, then, ye requested that we would at large make you acquainted with what really took place, we have for the present sent you this summary account through our brother, Marcus. When, therefore, ye have yourselves read this Epistle, be pleased to send it to the brethren at a greater distance, that they also may glorify the Lord who makes such choice of His own servants. To Him who is able to bring us all by His grace and goodness into his everlasting kingdom, through His only-begotten Son Jesus Christ, to Him be glory, and honor, and power, and majesty, forever. Amen. Salute all the saints. They that are with us salute you, and Evarestus, who wrote this Epistle, with all his house.

Chapter XXI. The Date of the Martyrdom.

Now, the blessed Polycarp suffered martyrdom on the second day of the month Xanthicus just begun, the seventh day before the Kalends of May, on the great Sabbath, at the eighth hour. He was taken by Herod, Philip the Trallian being high priest, Statius Quadratus being proconsul, but Jesus Christ being King forever, to whom be glory, honor, majesty, and an everlasting throne, from generation to generation. Amen.

Chapter XXII. Salutation.

We wish you, brethren, all happiness, while you walk according to the doctrine of the Gospel of Jesus Christ, with whom be glory to God the Father and the Holy Spirit, for the salvation of His holy elect, after whose example the blessed Polycarp suffered, following in whose steins may we too be found in the kingdom of Jesus Christ!

These things Caius transcribed from the copy of Irenæus (who was a disciple of Polycarp), having himself been intimate with Irenæus. And I, Socrates, transcribed them at Corinth from the copy of Caius. Grace be with you all.

And I again, Pionius, wrote them from the previously written copy, having carefully searched into them, and the blessed Polycarp having manifested them to me through a revelation, even as I shall show in what follows. I have collected these things, when they had almost faded away through the lapse of time, that the Lord Jesus Christ may also gather me along with His elect into His heavenly kingdom, to whom, with the Father and the Holy Spirit, be glory forever and ever. Amen.[2]

NOTES

1. This episode is recorded in the 2nd century treatise of Irenæus of Lyons entitled *Against Heresies*, Book III, Chapter 3, which may be found in *The Ante-Nicene Christian Library, Volume 2: Justin Martyr and Irenæus*.
2. This English version of *The Encyclical Epistle to the Church at Smyrna Concerning the Martyrdom of the Holy Polycarp* is taken from *Ante-Nicene Fathers, Volume I: The Apostolic Fathers*, translated by Alexander Roberts and James Donaldson.

Chapter 4

The Passion of Justin Martyr and Companions

Not long after the death of Saint Polycarp, another remarkable martyrdom took place in Rome. Saint Justin Martyr was born in Samaria, most likely to a family of Greco-Roman gentile origin. As a youth, he embraced the pagan philosophies of the day, but finding none of them satisfactory, came to accept and reverence Christian theology. He credited the heroic deaths of the early Christians as playing a key role in his conversion, saying: "When I was a disciple of Plato, hearing the accusations made against the Christians and seeing them intrepid in the face of death and of all that men fear, I said to myself that it was impossible that they should be living in evil and in the love of pleasure." [1]

Justin would go on to found a school of philosophy in Rome and write voluminous Christian apologetical works, a few of which survive to this day. During the reign of Marcus Aurelius, Justin was denounced by the pagan philosopher, Crescens, and made to stand trial before Junius Rusticus, a successful general, urban prefect of Rome, and a noted philosopher in his own right.

Justin's martyrdom took place about the year AD 165. This account of his trial and execution in company with several others is considered one of the most ancient and reliable of the martyrdom accounts to have survived antiquity. The dialogue below between Saint Justin and Rusticus may have been taken from actual transcripts of the trial.

The Martyrdom of the Holy Martyrs Justin, Chariton, Charites, Pæon, and Liberianus, Who Suffered at Rome.

Chapter I. Examination of Justin by the Prefect.

In the time of the lawless partisans of idolatry, wicked decrees were passed against the godly Christians in town and country to force them to offer libations to vain idols. And accordingly the holy men, having been apprehended, were brought before the prefect of Rome, Rusticus by name. And when they had been brought before his judgment-seat, said to Justin, "Obey the gods at once and submit to the kings."

Justin said, "To obey the commandments of our Savior Jesus Christ is worthy neither of blame nor of condemnation."

Rusticus the prefect said, "What kind of doctrines do you profess?"

Justin said, "I have endeavored to learn all doctrines, but I have acquiesced at last in the true doctrines, those namely of the Christians, even though they do not please those who hold false opinions."

Rusticus the prefect said, "Are those the doctrines that please you, you utterly wretched man?"

Justin said, "Yes, since I adhere to them with right dogma."

Rusticus the prefect said, "What is the dogma?"

Justin said, "That according to which we worship the God of the Christians, whom we reckon to be one from the beginning, the maker and fashioner of the whole creation, visible and invisible. And the Lord Jesus Christ, the Son of God, who had also been preached beforehand by the prophets as about to be present with the race of men, the herald of salvation and teacher of good disciples. And I, being a man, think that what I can say is insignificant in comparison with His boundless divinity, acknowledging a certain prophetic power, since it was prophesied concerning Him of whom now I say that He is the Son of God. For I know that of old the prophets foretold His appearance among men."

Chapter II. Examination of Justin Continued.

Rusticus the prefect said, "Where do you assemble?"

Justin said, "Where each one chooses and can: for do you fancy that we all meet in the very same place? Not so, because the God of the Christians is not circumscribed by place, but being invisible, fills heaven and earth, and everywhere is worshipped and glorified by the faithful."

Rusticus the prefect said, "Tell me where you assemble, or into what place do you collect your followers?"

Justin said, "I live above one Martinus at the Timiotinian Bath, and during the whole time (and I am now living in Rome for the second time) I am unaware of any other meeting than his. And if any one wished to come to me, I communicated to him the doctrines of truth."

Rusticus said, "Are you not, then, a Christian?"

Justin said, "Yes, I am a Christian."

Chapter III. Examination of Chariton and Others.

Then said the prefect Rusticus to Chariton, "Tell me further, Chariton, are you also a Christian?"

Chariton said, "I am a Christian by the command of God."

Rusticus the prefect asked the woman Charito, "What say you, Charito?"

Charito said, "I am a Christian by the grace of God."

Rusticus said to Euelpistus, "And what are you?"

Euelpistus, a servant of Cæsar, answered, "I too am a Christian, having been freed by Christ, and by the grace of Christ I partake of the same hope."

Rusticus the prefect said to Hierax, "And you, are you a Christian?"

Hierax said, "Yes, I am a Christian, for I revere and worship the same God."

Rusticus the prefect said, "Did Justin make you Christians?"

Hierax said, "I was a Christian, and will be a Christian."

And Pæon stood up and said, "I too am a Christian."

Rusticus the prefect said, "Who taught you?"

Pæon said, "From our parents we received this good confession."

Euelpistus said, "I willingly heard the words of Justin. But from my parents also I learned to be a Christian."

Rusticus the prefect said, "Where are your parents?"

Euelpistus said, "In Cappadocia."

Rusticus says to Hierax, "Where are your parents?"

And he answered and said, "Christ is our true father, and faith in Him is our mother. And my earthly parents died, and I, when I was driven from Iconium in Phrygia, came here."

Rusticus the prefect said to Liberianus, "And what say you? Are you a Christian and unwilling to worship [the gods]?"

Liberianus said, "I too am a Christian, for I worship and reverence the only true God."

Chapter IV. Rusticus Threatens the Christians with Death.

The prefect says to Justin, "Hearken, you who are called learned, and think that you know true doctrines: if you are scourged and beheaded, do you believe you will ascend into heaven?"

Justin said, "I hope that if I endure these things, I shall have His gifts. For I know that to all who have thus lived, there abides the divine favor until the completion of the whole world."

Rusticus the prefect said, "Do you suppose, then, that you will ascend into heaven to receive some recompense?"

Justin said, "I do not suppose it, but I know and am fully persuaded of it."

Rusticus the prefect said, "Let us, then, now come to the matter in hand and which presses. Having come together, offer sacrifice with one accord to the gods."

Justin said, "No right-thinking person falls away from piety to impiety."

Rusticus the prefect said, "Unless ye obey, ye shall be mercilessly punished."

Justin said, "Through prayer we can be saved on account of our Lord Jesus Christ even when we have been punished, because this shall become to us salvation and confidence at the more fearful and universal judgment-seat of our Lord and Savior."

Thus also said the other martyrs: "Do what you will, for we are Christians and do not sacrifice to idols."

Chapter V. Sentence Pronounced and Executed.

Rusticus the prefect pronounced sentence, saying, "Let those who have refused to sacrifice to the gods and to yield to the command of the emperor be scourged, and led away to suffer the punishment of decapitation, according to the laws."

The holy martyrs having glorified God and having gone forth to the accustomed place, were beheaded and perfected their testimony in the confession of the Savior. And some of the faithful having secretly removed their bodies, laid them in a suitable place, the grace of our Lord Jesus Christ having wrought along with them, to whom be glory for ever and ever. Amen.[2]

NOTES

1. Taken from the *Second Apology* of Saint Justin Martyr, Chapter 12.
2. This English translation of *The Martyrdom of the Holy Martyrs Justin, Chariton, Charites, Pæon and Liberianus who Suffered at Rome* was prepared by M. Dods and originally appeared in *The Ante-Nicene Christian Library, Volume 2: Justin Martyr and Athenagoras.*

Chapter 5

The Apology and Acts of Apollonius

Little is known of Saint Apollonius, the subject of the next account. Aside from his apology and subsequent execution for the crime of being a Christian, he is mentioned in the Ecclesiastical History of Eusebius as well as a 5th century catalogue of illustrious men compiled by Saint Jerome.[1] In this latter source, Apollonius is named a Roman senator who was denounced as a Christian by a slave during the reign of Commodus. Early tradition makes AD 185 the year of his death.

The passage below is a translation of an ancient account recorded in the Armenian language. Though the original was known to Eusebius and Jerome, it was believed lost until an ancient manuscript containing this version in Armenian was discovered in Venice in 1874.

Unlike many of the other martyrdom accounts offered in this book, this one contains several extended apologetical passages where Apollonius is allowed to expound upon his reasons for faith. According to Jerome, the martyr recited these tracts from a work that he had previously written. This latitude granted by the Senate would make sense if Apollonius were, in fact, a member of that august body.

The Apology and Acts of Apollonius

Christ, Who giveth all things, prepareth a crown of righteousness for those who are well-minded and stand firm by the faith in God.

I AM A CHRISTIAN

For the chosen ones of God are called to this righteousness, in order that, having fought the good fight with fortitude, they may attain the promises which God, Who lies not, hath promised to those who love Him and believe in Him with their whole soul. One of these also was the blessed martyr and goodly champion of Christ, Apollonius. He had lived a good and ascetic life in the great Rome, and, desirous of the earnest of his heavenly call, he was numbered among the holy martyrs of Christ.

The blessed one bore witness before the Senate and Perennius the Prefect, and gave his answers with great boldness, whose memorials are as follows:

Perennius, the Prefect, commanded that he should be brought before the Senate and said to him, "O Apollonius, wherefore dost thou resist the invincible laws and decree of the Emperors and dost refuse to sacrifice to the gods?"

Apollonius said, "Because I am a Christian. Therefore, I fear God Who made heaven and earth and sacrifice not to empty idols."

The Prefect said, "But thou ought to repent of this mind of thine because of the edicts of the Emperors and take oath by the good fortune of the autocrat, Commodus."

Apollonius replied, "Hear with understanding this my answer. He who repents of just and good works, in truth such a man is godless and without hope. But he who repents of lawless deeds and of evil thoughts and returns not again to them, such a one is a lover of God and hath regard to the hope. And I now am firmly resolved in this my mind to keep the beautiful and glorious command of God, which He taught by my Lord Christ, Who knows the thoughts of men and beholds whatsoever is done in secret or in the open.

"It is best to swear not at all, but in all things to live in peace and truth. For a great oath is the truth, and for this reason is it a bad and an ill thing to swear by Christ. But because of falsehood is there disbelief, and because of disbelief there is swearing. I am willing to swear in truth by the true God that we, too, love the

Emperor and offer up prayers for his Majesty."

The Prefect said, "Come, then, and sacrifice to Apollo and to the other gods and to the Emperor's image."

Apollonius said, "As to my change of mind, and as to the oath, I have given thee answer. But as to sacrifices, I and all Christians offer a bloodless sacrifice to God, Lord of heaven and earth, and of the sea, and of every living being, in behalf of the spiritual and rational images who have been appointed by the providence of God to rule over the earth. Wherefore, according to the command of the God-given precept, we make our prayers to Him Who dwells in Heaven, Who is the only God, that they may justly rule upon this earth, knowing for certain that he [Commodus] also is established Emperor through none other but only through the one King, God, Who holds everyone in His hand."

The Prefect said, "Surely thou wast not summoned hither to talk philosophy. I will give thee one day's respite, that thou mayest consider thine interest and advise thyself concerning thy life." And he ordered him to be taken to prison.

And after three days he commanded him to be brought forward and said to him, "What counsel hast thou formed for thyself?"

Apollonius answered, "To remain firm in my religion, as I told thee before."

The Prefect said, "Because of the decree of the Senate I advise thee to repent and to sacrifice to the gods to whom all the earth gives homage and sacrifices, for it is far better for thee to live among us than to die a miserable death. Methinks thou art not unacquainted with the decree of the Senate."

Apollonius said "I know the command of the Omnipotent God, and I remain firm in my religion, and I do no homage to idols made with hands, which have been fashioned of gold and silver and wood, and which neither see nor hear because they are the work of men's hands, and they know not the true service of God. But I have learnt to adore the heavenly God and to do homage to Him alone, Who breathed the breath of life into all men and continually dispenses life unto all. And I will not again debase myself and cast myself down into the pit. For it is a great shame to do homage to vile things, and it is a servile action to adore what is vain. And men sin in adoring such things. Foolish were those who invented them, and yet more senseless they that adore them and honor them.

"The Egyptians do homage to an onion in their folly. The Athenians unto this very day make and adore the head of an ox in copper, which they call the good fortune of Athens. And this they have even set up in a conspicuous place near to the statue of Zeus and Heracles, in order that they may pray to them. And yet what more is this than dried clay or a baked potsherd? Eyes have they, and see not. Ears have they, and hear not. Hands they have, but draw not things to themselves. Feet have they, and walk not. For the mere form bestows not real substance, and I think that Socrates also was making ridicule of the Athenians when he swore by the poplar tree, and by the dog, and by dry wood. In the first place, men sin against themselves by worshipping them. In the second place, they are guilty of impiety towards God, because they do not know the truth.

"The Egyptians, again, have given the name of God to the onion, and to a wooden mortar, and to the fruits of the field which we feed upon and which enter the belly and pass out into the sweepings. These things have they adored. Aye, and they do homage to a fish, and to the dove, and to the dog, and to a stone, and a wolf. And they worship every one of them, the fictions of their own minds. In the third place, men sin whenever they pay homage to men and to angels and to demons, naming them gods."

The Prefect answered, "You have philosophized enough and have filled us with admiration. But dost thou not know this, O Apollonius, that it is the decree of the Senate that no one shall be named a Christian anywhere at all?"

Apollonius answered: "Aye, but it is not possible for a human decree of the Senate to prevail over the decree of God. For so far as men frivolously hate those who benefit them and slay them, just in this wise in many ways men stand aloof from God. But know thou this, that God has appointed death, and after death judgment upon all, over kings and poor men, rulers and slaves and freemen, and philosophers and ignorant men. But there is a distinction of death (from death). For this reason the disciples of Christ do daily die, torturing their desires, and mortifying them according to the Divine Scriptures. For we have no part at all in dissolute desires, nor do we allow impure sights, nor a lewd glance, nor an ear that listens to evil, lest our souls be wounded thereby. But since we live such a fair life, and exercise such good resolutions, we think it no hardship to die for the true God. For whatsoever we are, we are because of God, and for Him we endure tortures, that we may not die miserably the everlasting death. And moreover we do not resent having our goods taken from us, because we know that whether we live or whether we die, we are the Lord's. Fever or jaundice or any other disease can slay a man. I may expect to die from one or the other of these."

The Prefect said, "Art thou bent upon death?"

Apollonius answered, "It is my desire to live in Christ, but I have no fear of death because of any love of life. For there is not anything that is more estimable than the life eternal, which is the source of deathlessness for the soul that hath lived here a noble life."

The Prefect said, "I do not understand thy meaning."

Apollonius said, "And what can I do for thee? For the Word of God illumines the heart, as the light gives sight to our eyes."

A certain philosopher who was at hand said, "O Apollonius, thou dost insult thyself, for thou art gone exceedingly astray although though dost even think to speak profound truths."

Apollonius said, "I have learnt to pray and not to insult, but thy dissembling bears witness to the blindness of thy heart, for the truth appears to be an insult only to the senseless."

The magistrate said, "Tell me plainly what thou didst mean."

Apollonius answered "The Word of God, the Savior of souls and of bodies, became man in Judæa and fulfilled all righteousness and was filled gloriously with Divine wisdom, and taught a pure religion, such as beseemed the sons of men, and to put to silence the beginning of sins. For He taught us to pacify anger, to moderate desire, to abate and diminish appetite, to put away sorrow, to take part in pity, to increase love, to cast away vain-glory, to abstain from taking vengeance, not to be vindictive, to despise death, not indeed from lawlessness, but as bearing with the lawless, to obey the laws of God, to reverence rulers, to worship God, to intrust the Spirit to immortal God, to look forward to judgment after death, to expect rewards after the resurrection to be given by God to those who have lived in piety.

"Teaching all this by word and deed, along with great firmness and glorified by all for the benefits which He conferred on them, He was slain at last, as were also before Him philosophers and just men. For the just are seen to be a cause of offence to the unjust. As also the Divine Scripture saith: 'We will bind the just man, because he was a cause of offence to us,'[2] but also one of the Greek philosophers said: 'The just man shall be tortured, he shall be spat upon, and last of all he shall be crucified.'[3] Just as the Athenians passed an unjust sentence of death and charged him falsely because they yielded to the mob, so also our Savior was at last sentenced to death by the lawless: by the lawless who were filled with envy and malice against Him, as also against the prophets who were before Him, who spake beforehand concerning Him thus: 'He shall come and shall do good unto all and shall persuade all men by His goodness even to worship God the Father and Maker of all,' in Whom also we believe, rendering homage, because we learned from Him pure commandments, which we knew not and, therefore, we are no longer in error but, having lived a good life, we await the hope to come."

The magistrate said, "I thought that thou wast changed in the night from that mind of thine."

Apollonius said, "And I expected that thy thoughts would be changed in the night and the eyes of thy spirit be opened by my answer, and that thy heart would bear fruit, and that thou wouldst worship God, the Creator of all, and unto Him continually offer thy prayers by means of compassion. For compassion shown to men by men is a bloodless sacrifice and holy unto God."

The magistrate said, "I would fain let thee go, but I cannot because of the decree of the Senate. Yet with benevolence I pronounce sentence on thee." And he ordered him to be beheaded with a sword.

Apollonius said, "I thank my God for thy sentence."

And the executioners straightway led him away and beheaded him while he continued to glorify the Father and Son and Holy Spirit, to Whom be glory for ever. Amen.[4]

NOTES

1. This mention of Apollonius may be found in *Saint Jerome: On Illustrious Men*, Chapter 42: Apollonius the Senator as translated into English by Thomas P. Halton.
2. See Chapter 1, note 4.
3. This quote is taken from *The Republic* of Plato, Book II, Section 361e.
4. This rendering in English of The Apology and Acts of Apollonius was done by F. C. Conybeare and may be found in *The Armenian Apology and Acts of Apollonius and Other Monuments of the Early Church*.

Chapter 6

The Scillitan Martyrs

The accounts offered to this point have all taken place in centers of early Christian activity from the very beginning. The following very brief account comes down to us from the more distant provinces of Roman Africa. This group of martyrs originated from the town of Scillium in the interior and were taken to Carthage for trial before the Roman proconsul, Vigellius Saturninus. It is believed that the trial and execution of the martyrs took place in the year AD 180 or slightly after.

This text is unique in several ways. It is the most ancient of martyrdom accounts to have originated from Roman Africa. Indeed, it is the oldest extant Christian document of any kind from the Roman African provinces to have survived antiquity. In addition, it is composed almost entirely of dialogue between the proconsul and the martyrs, with only abbreviated introductory and concluding remarks and no information at all regarding the authorship. This means that what you read below is very likely the official court transcript of the trial of the martyrs.

Of particular note is the willingness of the martyrs to proclaim themselves as Christians, knowing as they did so that such a declaration carried a death sentence. The proconsul appears less as a tyrant than a fair Roman magistrate who gives the defendants every opportunity to adhere to the law. However, when they persist in their confession of Christ, he does what Roman judges were expected to do: execute the law without hesitation or emotion.

✢ ✤ ✢

I AM A CHRISTIAN

The Passion of the Scillitan Martyrs

When Præsens, for the second time, and Claudianus were the consuls, on the seventeenth day of July, at Carthage, there were set in the judgment-hall Speratus, Nartzalus, Cittinus, Donata, Secunda and Vestia.

Saturninus the proconsul said: "You can win the indulgence of our lord the Emperor if you return to a sound mind."

Speratus said: "We have never done ill, we have not lent ourselves to wrong, we have never spoken ill, but when ill-treated we have given thanks, because we pay heed to our Emperor."

Saturninus the proconsul said: "We too are religious, and our religion is simple, and we swear by the genius of our lord the Emperor, and pray for his welfare, as ye also ought to do."

Speratus said: "If thou wilt peaceably lend me thine ears, I can tell thee the mystery of simplicity."

Saturninus said: "I will not lend mine ears to thee, when you begin to speak evil things of our sacred rites. But rather swear thou by the genius of our lord the Emperor."

Speratus said: "The empire of this world I know not, but rather I serve that God, whom no man hath seen, nor with these eyes can see. I have committed no theft, but if I have bought anything I pay the tax because I know my Lord, the King of kings and Emperor of all nations."

Saturninus the proconsul said to the rest: "Cease to be of this persuasion."

Speratus said: "It is an ill persuasion to do murder, to speak false witness."

Saturninus the proconsul said: "Be not partakers of this folly."

Cittinus said: "We have none other to fear, save only our Lord God, who is in heaven."

Donata said: "Honor to Cæsar as Cæsar, but fear to God."

Vestia said: "I am a Christian."

Secunda said: "What I am, that I wish to be."

Saturninus the proconsul said to Speratus: "Do you persist in being a Christian?"

Speratus said: "I am a Christian." And with him they all agreed.

Saturninus the proconsul said: "Will ye have a space to consider?"

Speratus said: "In a matter so straightforward there is no considering."

Saturninus the proconsul said: "What are the things in your chest?"

Speratus said: "Books and epistles of Paul, a just man."

Saturninus the proconsul said: "Have a delay of thirty days and bethink yourselves."

Speratus said a second time: "I am a Christian." And with him they all agreed.

Saturninus the proconsul read out the decree from the tablet: "Speratus, Nartzalus, Cittinus, Donata, Vestia, Secunda and the rest having confessed that they live according to the Christian rite. Since after opportunity offered them of returning to the custom of the Romans they have obstinately persisted, it is determined that they be put to the sword."

Speratus said: "We give thanks to God."

Nartzalus said: "Today we are martyrs in heaven. Thanks be to God."

Saturninus the proconsul ordered it to be declared by the herald: "Speratus, Nartzalus, Cittinus, Veturius, Felix, Aquilinus, Lætantius, Januaria, Generosa, Vestia, Donata and Secunda, I have ordered to be executed."

They all said: "Thanks be to God."

And so they all together were crowned with martyrdom. And they reign with the Father and the Son and the Holy Ghost, forever and ever. Amen.[1]

NOTES

1. This translation of The Passion of the Scillitan Martyrs was completed by A. Robinson and included in *The Ante-Nicene Fathers, Volume IX*.

CHAPTER 7

The Passion of Saints Perpetua, Felicitas, and Companions

On March 7, AD 203, during the reign of the emperor Septimius Severus, five Christians were martyred in the amphitheater of Carthage. The three men were named Revocatus, Saturus, and Saturninus. The two women, however, are more famous, having their names entered into the Roman Canon of the Mass: Felicitas, a slave eight months pregnant when she entered into prison, and Perpetua, a young Roman matron of noble birth who had recently given birth.

The antiquity and authenticity of the Passion of Perpetua and Felicitas *is not seriously challenged by most scholars. Indeed, large parts of the work seem to have been written or dictated by Perpetua herself, with only the brief introduction and the climax of the martyrdom showing the pen of a first-hand observer. Some have speculated that this observer may have been the prolific Christian apologist and polemicist, Tertullian, who lived in Roman north Africa at about the same time.*

Unlike the previous martyrdom accounts in this book, this passion contains passages describing the plight of the martyrs while in prison awaiting the festival day when they would do battle with wild beasts in the amphitheater. Of special note are the visions experienced by Perpetua and Saturus while in prison. In one of her visions, Perpetua meets her departed younger brother, Dinocrates. This is one of the earliest extra-biblical references to the Catholic belief in the transitional state of Purgatory where the prayers of the living may ease the sufferings of souls

I AM A CHRISTIAN

being purified before entering the heavenly kingdom.

It should also be noted that though the persecution during which Perpetua and Felicitas were slain occurred during the reign of Septimius Severus, it is thought to have been a local persecution only, not empire-wide. The reputation of Severus is quite mixed when it comes to his attitude toward Christianity. The unreliable Historia Augusta *records that he promulgated an edict making it illegal to convert to Judaism or Christianity.*[1] *Meanwhile, the aforementioned Tertullian, writing in* AD *212 (or 217) in his* Letter to Scapula *admits that though persecutions had taken place under Severus, that emperor was: "graciously mindful of the Christians...Both women and men of highest rank, whom Severus knew well to be Christians, were not merely permitted by him to remain uninjured, but he even bore distinguished testimony in their favor, and gave them publicly back to us from the hands of a raging populace."*[2]

THE PASSION OF THE HOLY MARTYRS PERPETUA AND FELICITAS

Preface

If ancient illustrations of faith which both testify to God's grace and tend to man's edification are collected in writing, so that by the perusal of them, as if by the reproduction of the facts, as well God may be honored as man may be strengthened. Why should not new instances be also collected that shall be equally suitable for both purposes, if only on the ground that these modern examples will one day become ancient and available for posterity, although in their present time they are esteemed of less authority by reason of the presumed veneration for antiquity?

But let men look to it if they judge the power of the Holy Spirit to be one according to the times and seasons. Since some things of later date must be esteemed of more account as being nearer to the very last times, in accordance with the exuberance of grace manifested to the final periods determined for the world. For, "In the last days," saith the Lord, "I will pour out of my Spirit upon all flesh, and their sons and their daughters shall prophesy. And upon my servants and my handmaidens will

The Passion of Saints Perpetua, Felicitas and Companions

I pour out of my Spirit, and your young men shall see visions, and your old men shall dream dreams."³ And thus we who both acknowledge and reverence, even as we do the prophecies, modern visions as equally promised to us and consider the other powers of the Holy Spirit as an agency of the Church for which also He was sent, administering all gifts in all, even as the Lord distributed to every one as well needfully collect them in writing, as commemorate them in reading to God's glory, that so no weakness or despondency of faith may suppose that the divine grace abode only among the ancients, whether in respect of the condescension that raised up martyrs or that gave revelations, since God always carries into effect what He has promised, for a testimony to unbelievers, to believers for a benefit. And we therefore, what we have heard and handled, declare also to you, brethren and little children, that as well you who were concerned in these matters may be reminded of them again to the glory of the Lord, as that you who know them by report may have communion with the blessed martyrs and through them with the Lord Jesus Christ, to whom be glory and honor, for ever and ever. Amen.

Chapter I.

The young catechumens, Revocatus and his fellow-servant Felicitas, Saturninus and Secundulus, were apprehended. And among them also was Vivia Perpetua, respectably born, liberally educated, a married matron, having a father and mother and two brothers, one of whom, like herself, was a catechumen, and a son an infant at the breast. She herself was about twenty-two years of age. From this point onward she shall herself narrate the whole course of her martyrdom, as she left it described by her own hand and with her own mind:

While we were still with the persecutors, and my father, for the sake of his affection for me, was persisting in seeking to turn me

I AM A CHRISTIAN

away and to cast me down from the faith, "Father," said I, "do you see, let us say, this vessel lying here to be a little pitcher, or something else?"

And he said, "I see it to be so."

And I replied to him, "Can it be called by any other name than what it is?"

And he said, "No."

"Neither can I call myself anything else than what I am, a Christian."

Then my father, provoked at this saying, threw himself upon me as if he would tear my eyes out. But he only distressed me and went away overcome by the devil's arguments. Then, in a few days after I had been without my father, I gave thanks to the Lord, and his absence became a source of consolation to me. In that same interval of a few days we were baptized, and to me the Spirit prescribed that in the water of baptism nothing else was to be sought for bodily endurance.

After a few days we are taken into the dungeon, and I was very much afraid because I had never felt such darkness. O terrible day! O the fierce heat of the shock of the soldiery, because of the crowds! I was very unusually distressed by my anxiety for my infant. There were present there Tertius and Pomponius, the blessed deacons who ministered to us and had arranged by means of a gratuity that we might be refreshed by being sent out for a few hours into a pleasanter part of the prison.

Then going out of the dungeon, all attended to their own wants. I suckled my child which was now enfeebled with hunger. In my anxiety for it, I addressed my mother and comforted my brother, and commended to their care my son. I was languishing because I had seen them languishing on my account. Such solicitude I suffered for many days, and I obtained for my infant to remain in the dungeon with me, and forthwith I grew strong and was relieved from distress and anxiety about my infant, and the dungeon became to me as it were a palace so that I preferred being there to being elsewhere.

Then my brother said to me, "My dear sister, you are already in a position of great dignity and are such that you may ask for a vision, and that it may be made known to you whether this is to result in a passion or an escape."

And I, who knew that I was privileged to converse with the Lord whose kindnesses I had found to be so great, boldly promised him and said, "Tomorrow I will tell you."

And I asked, and this was what was shown me. I saw a golden ladder of marvellous height reaching up even to heaven and very narrow, so that persons could only ascend it one by one. And on the sides of the ladder was fixed every kind of iron weapon. There were there swords, lances, hooks, daggers, so that if any one went up carelessly or not looking upwards, he would be torn to pieces and his flesh would cleave to the iron weapons. And under the ladder itself was crouching a dragon of wonderful size who lay in wait for those who ascended and frightened them from the ascent.

And Saturus went up first, who had subsequently delivered himself up freely on our account, not having been present at the time that we were taken prisoners. And he attained the top of the ladder and turned towards me, and said to me, "Perpetua, I am waiting for you, but be careful that the dragon does not bite you."

And I said, "In the name of the Lord Jesus Christ, he shall not hurt me."

And from under the ladder itself, as if in fear of me, he slowly lifted up his head, and as I trod upon the first step, I trod upon his head. And I went up, and I saw an immense extent of garden, and in the midst of the garden a white-haired man sitting in the dress of a shepherd of a large stature, milking sheep. And standing around were many thousand white-robed ones. And he raised his head and looked upon me and said to me, "Thou art welcome, daughter." And he called me, and from the cheese as he was milking he gave me as it were a little cake, and I received it with folded hands. And I ate it and all who stood around said, "Amen."

And at the sound of their voices I was awakened, still tasting a sweetness which I cannot describe. And I immediately related this to my brother, and we understood that it was to be a passion and we ceased henceforth to have any hope in this world.

Chapter II.

After a few days there prevailed a report that we should be heard. And then my father came to me from the city, worn out with anxiety. He came up to me, that he might cast me down saying, "Have pity, my daughter, on my grey hairs. Have pity on your father, if I am worthy to be called a father by you. If with these hands I have brought you up to this flower of your age, if I have preferred you to all your brothers, do not deliver me up to the scorn of men. Have regard to your brothers, have regard to your mother and your aunt, have regard to your son, who will not be able to live after you. Lay aside your courage and do not bring us all to destruction. For none of us will speak in freedom if you should suffer anything."

These things said my father in his affection, kissing my hands and throwing himself at my feet, and with tears he called me not Daughter, but Lady. And I grieved over the grey hairs of my father, that he alone of all my family would not rejoice over my passion. And I comforted him, saying, "On that scaffold whatever God wills shall happen. For know that we are not placed in our own power, but in that of God." And he departed from me in sorrow.

Another day while we were at dinner, we were suddenly taken away to be heard, and we arrived at the town-hall. At once the rumor spread through the neighborhood of the public place, and an immense number of people were gathered together. We mounted the platform. The rest were interrogated and confessed. Then they came to me, and my father immediately appeared with my boy and withdrew me from the step and said in a supplicating tone, "Have pity on your babe."

And Hilarianus the procurator, who had just received the power of life and death in the place of the proconsul Minucius Timinianus who was deceased said, "Spare the grey hairs of your father. Spare the infancy of your boy. Offer sacrifice for the well-being of the emperors."

And I replied, "I will not do so."

Hilarianus said, "Are you a Christian?"

And I replied, "I am a Christian."

And as my father stood there to cast me down from the faith, he was ordered by Hilarianus to be thrown down and was beaten with rods. And my father's misfortune grieved me as if I myself had been beaten, I so grieved for his wretched old age.

The procurator then delivers judgment on all of us and condemns us to the wild beasts, and we went down cheerfully to the dungeon. Then, because my child had been used to receive suck from me and to stay with me in the prison, I send Pomponius the deacon to my father to ask for the infant, but my father would not give it him. And even as God willed it, the child no longer desired the breast, nor did my breast cause me uneasiness, lest I should be tormented by care for my babe and by the pain of my breasts at once.

After a few days whilst we were all praying, on a sudden in the middle of our prayer, there came to me a word and I named Dinocrates. And I was amazed that that name had never come into my mind until then, and I was grieved as I remembered his misfortune. And I felt myself immediately to be worthy and to be called on to ask on his behalf. And for him I began earnestly to make supplication and to cry with groaning to the Lord. Without delay, on that very night, this was shown to me in a vision.[4]

I saw Dinocrates going out from a gloomy place where also there were several others, and he was parched and very thirsty with a filthy countenance and pallid color, and the wound on his face which he had when he died. This Dinocrates had been my brother after the flesh, seven years of age who died miserably with disease—his face being so eaten out with cancer, that his death caused repugnance to all men. For him I had made my prayer, and between him and me there was a large interval, so that neither of us could approach to the other. And moreover, in the same place where Dinocrates was, there was a pool full of water, having its brink higher than was the stature of the boy, and Dinocrates raised himself up as if to drink. And I was grieved that, although that pool held water, still on account of the height to its brink, he could not drink. And I was aroused and knew that my brother was in suffering. But I trusted that my prayer would bring help to his suffering, and I prayed for him every day until we passed over into the prison of the camp, for we were to fight in the camp-show. Then was the birthday of Geta Cæsar, and I made my prayer for my brother day and night, groaning and weeping that he might be granted to me.

Then, on the day on which we remained in fetters, this was shown to me. I saw that that place which I had formerly observed to be in gloom was now bright, and Dinocrates, with a clean body well clad, was finding refreshment. And where there had been a wound, I saw a scar. And that pool which I had before seen, I saw now with its margin lowered even to the boy's navel. And one drew water from the pool incessantly, and upon its brink was a goblet filled with water. And Dinocrates drew near and began to drink from it, and the goblet did not fail. And when he was satisfied, he went away from the water to play joyously after the manner of children, and I awoke. Then I understood that he was translated from the place of punishment.

Chapter III.

Again, after a few days, Pudens, a soldier, an assistant overseer of the prison, who began to regard us in great esteem, perceiving that the great power of God was in us, admitted many brethren to see us, that both we and they might be mutually refreshed. And when the day of the exhibition drew near, my father, worn with suffering, came in to me and began to tear out his beard, and to throw himself on the earth, and to cast himself down on his face, and to reproach his years, and to utter such words as might move all creation. I grieved for his unhappy old age.

The day before that on which we were to fight, I saw in a vision that Pomponius the deacon came hither to the gate of the prison and knocked vehemently. I went out to him and opened the gate for him, and he was clothed in a richly ornamented white robe, and he had on manifold *callicula*. And he said to me, "Perpetua, we are waiting for you. Come!" And he held his hand to me, and we began to go through rough and winding places.

Scarcely at length had we arrived breathless at the amphitheater, when he led me into the middle of the arena and said to me, "Do not fear, I am here with you, and I am laboring with you," and he departed. And I gazed upon an immense assembly in astonishment. And because I knew that I was given to the wild beasts, I marvelled that the wild beasts were not let loose upon me. Then there came forth against me a certain Egyptian, horrible in appearance, with his backers, to fight with me. And there came to me handsome youths as my helpers and encouragers, and I was stripped and became a man.

Then my helpers began to rub me with oil, as is the custom for contest, and I beheld that Egyptian on the other hand rolling in the dust. And a certain man came forth of wondrous height so that he even over-topped the top of the amphitheater. And he wore a loose tunic and a purple robe between two bands over the middle of the breast, and he had on *callicula* of varied form, made of gold and silver, and he carried a rod as if he were a trainer of gladiators, and a green branch upon which were apples of gold. And he called for silence, and said, "This Egyptian, if he should overcome this woman, shall kill her with the sword. And if she shall conquer him, she shall receive this branch." Then he departed.

And we drew near to one another and began to deal out blows. He sought to lay hold of my feet, while I struck at his face with my heels, and I was lifted up in the air and began thus to thrust at him as if spurning the earth. But when I saw that there was some delay I joined my hands so as to twine my fingers with one another, and I took hold upon his head, and he fell on his face, and I trod upon his head. And the people began to shout, and my backers to exult. And I drew near to the trainer and took the branch, and he kissed me and said to me, "Daughter, peace be with you." And I began to go gloriously to the Sanavivarian gate.

Then I awoke and perceived that I was not to fight with beasts, but against the devil. Still I knew that the victory was awaiting me. This, so far, I have completed several days before the exhibition, but what passed at the exhibition itself let who will write.

Chapter IV.

Moreover, also, the blessed Saturus related this his vision, which he himself committed to writing:

We had suffered and we were gone forth from the flesh, and we were beginning to be borne by four angels into the east, and their hands touched us not. And we floated not supine, looking upwards, but as if ascending a gentle slope. And being set free, we at length saw the first boundless light, and I said, "Perpetua," (for she was at my side), "this is what the Lord promised to us. We have received the promise."

And while we are borne by those same four angels, there appears to us a vast space which was like a pleasure-garden, having rose-trees and every kind of flower. And the height of the trees was after the measure of a cypress, and their leaves were falling incessantly. Moreover, there in the pleasure-garden four other angels appeared, brighter than the previous ones, who when they saw us, gave us honor and said to the rest of the angels, "Here they are! Here they are!" with admiration. And those four angels who bore us, being greatly afraid, put us down, and we passed over on foot the space of a furlong in a broad path. There we found Jocundus and Saturninus and Artaxius, who having suffered the same persecution were burnt alive, and Quintus who also himself a martyr had departed in the prison. And we asked of them where the rest were. And the angels said to us, "Come first, enter and greet your Lord."

And we came near the place, the walls of which were such as if they were built of light. And before the gate of that place stood four angels who clothed those who entered with white robes.

And being clothed, we entered and saw the boundless light and heard the united voice of some who said without ceasing, "Holy! Holy! Holy!"

And in the midst of that place we saw as it were a hoary man sitting, having snow-white hair and with a youthful countenance. And his feet we saw not. And on his right hand and on his left were four-and-twenty elders, and behind them a great many others were standing. We entered with great wonder and stood before the throne. And the four angels raised us up, and we kissed Him, and He passed His hand over our face. And the rest of the elders said to us, "Let us stand." And we stood and made peace. And the elders said to us, "Go and enjoy."

And I said, "Perpetua, you have what you wish."

And she said to me, "Thanks be to God, that joyous as I was in the flesh, I am now more joyous here."

And we went forth and saw before the entrance Optatus the bishop at the right hand, and Aspasius the presbyter, a teacher, at the left hand, separate and sad. And they cast themselves at our feet and said to us, "Restore peace between us, because you have gone forth and have left us thus."

And we said to them, "Art not thou our father, and thou our presbyter, that you should cast yourselves at our feet?" And we prostrated ourselves and we embraced them, and Perpetua began to speak with them, and we drew them apart in the pleasure-garden under a rose-tree.

And while we were speaking with them, the angels said unto them, "Let them alone, that they may refresh themselves. And if you have any dissensions between you, forgive one another."

And they drove them away. And they said to Optatus, "Rebuke thy people, because they assemble to you as if returning from the circus, and contending about factious matters."

And then it seemed to us as if they would shut the doors. And in that place we began to recognize many brethren, and moreover martyrs. We were all nourished with an indescribable odor, which satisfied us. Then, I joyously awoke.

Chapter V.

The above were the more eminent visions of the blessed martyrs Saturus and Perpetua themselves, which they themselves committed to writing. But God called Secundulus while he was yet in the prison by an earlier exit from the world, not without favor, so as to give a respite to the beasts. Nevertheless, even if his soul did not acknowledge cause for thankfulness, assuredly his flesh did.

But respecting Felicitas (for to her also the Lord's favor approached in the same way), when she had already gone eight months with child (for she had been pregnant when she was apprehended), as the day of the exhibition was drawing near, she was in great grief lest on account of her pregnancy she should be delayed—because pregnant women are not allowed to be publicly punished—and lest she should shed her sacred and guiltless blood among some who had been wicked subsequently. Moreover, also, her fellow-martyrs were painfully saddened lest they should leave so excellent a friend, and as it were companion, alone in the path of the same hope.

Therefore, joining together their united cry, they poured forth their prayer to the Lord three days before the exhibition. Immediately after their prayer her pains came upon her and when with the difficulty natural to an eight months' delivery, in the labor of bringing forth she was sorrowing, some one of the servants of the Cataractarii said to her, "You who are in such suffering now, what will you do when you are thrown to the beasts which you despised when you refused to sacrifice?"

And she replied, "Now it is I that suffer what I suffer, but then there will be another in me who will suffer for me, because I also am about to suffer for Him." Thus she brought forth a little girl which a certain sister brought up as her daughter.

Since then the Holy Spirit permitted, and by permitting willed, that the proceedings of that exhibition should be committed to writing, although we are unworthy to complete the description of so great a glory. Yet we obey as it were the command of the most blessed Perpetua, nay her sacred trust, and add one more testimony concerning her constancy and her loftiness of mind. While they were treated with more severity by the tribune because, from the intimations of certain deceitful men, he feared lest they should be withdrawn from the prison by some sort of magic incantations, Perpetua answered to his face and said, "Why do you not at least permit us to be refreshed, being as we are objectionable to the most noble Cæsar, and having to fight on his birthday? Or is it not your glory if we are brought forward fatter on that occasion?"

The tribune shuddered and blushed and commanded that they should be kept with more humanity, so that permission was given to their brethren and others to go in and be refreshed with them, even the keeper of the prison trusting them now himself.

Moreover, on the day before, when in that last meal which they call the free meal, they were partaking as far as they could, not of a free supper, but of an agape,[5] with the same firmness they were uttering such words as these to the people, denouncing against them the judgment of the Lord, bearing witness to the felicity of their passion, laughing at the curiosity of the people who came together, while Saturus said, "Tomorrow is not enough for you, for you to behold with pleasure that which you hate. Friends today, enemies tomorrow. Yet note our faces diligently, that you may recognize them on that day of judgment." Thus all departed thence astonished, and from these things many believed.

Chapter VI.

The day of their victory shone forth and they proceeded from the prison into the amphitheater as if to an assembly, joyous and of brilliant countenances, if perchance shrinking, it was with joy and not with fear. Perpetua followed with placid look, and with step and gait as a matron of Christ, beloved of God, casting down the luster of her eyes from the gaze of all. Moreover, Felicitas, rejoicing that she had safely brought forth so that she might fight with the wild beasts—from the blood and from the midwife to the gladiator, to wash after childbirth with a second baptism.

And when they were brought to the gate and were constrained to put on the clothing—the men that of the priests of Saturn, and the women that of those who were consecrated to Ceres—that noble-minded woman resisted even to the end with constancy. For she said, "We have come thus far of our own accord for this reason, that our liberty might not be restrained. For this reason we have yielded our minds, that we might not do any such thing as this. We have agreed on this with you."

Injustice acknowledged the justice. The tribune yielded to their being brought as simply as they were. Perpetua sang psalms, already treading under foot the head of the Egyptian. Revocatus and Saturninus and Saturus uttered threatenings against the gazing people about this martyrdom. When they came within sight of Hilarianus, by gesture and nod, they began to say to Hilarianus, "Thou judgest us," say they, "but God will judge thee." At this the people, exasperated, demanded that they should be tormented with scourges as they passed along the rank of the venators. And they indeed rejoiced that they should have incurred any one of their Lord's passions.

But He who had said, "Ask, and ye shall receive," gave to them when they asked, that death which each one had wished for. For when at any time they had been discoursing among themselves about their wish in respect of their martyrdom, Saturninus indeed had professed that he wished that he might be thrown to all the beasts, doubtless that he might wear a more glorious crown. Therefore in the beginning of the exhibition he and Revocatus made trial of the leopard, and moreover upon the scaffold they were harassed by the bear. Saturus, however, held nothing in greater abomination than a bear, but he imagined that he would be put an end to with one bite of a leopard. Therefore, when a wild boar was supplied, it was the huntsman rather who had supplied that boar who was gored by that same beast, and died the day after the shows. Saturus only was drawn out, and when he had been bound on the floor near to a bear, the bear would not come forth from his den. And so Saturus for the second time is recalled unhurt.

Moreover, for the young women the devil prepared a very fierce cow, provided especially for that purpose contrary to custom, rivalling their sex also in that of the beasts. And so, stripped and clothed with nets, they were led forth. The populace shuddered as they saw one young woman of delicate frame, and another with breasts still dropping from her recent childbirth. So, being recalled, they are unbound.

Perpetua is first led in. She was tossed and fell on her loins, and when she saw her tunic torn from her side, she drew it over her as a veil for her middle, rather mindful of her modesty than her suffering. Then she was called for again and bound up her dishevelled hair, for it was not becoming for a martyr to suffer with dishevelled hair lest she should appear to be mourning in her glory. So she rose up, and when she saw Felicitas crushed, she approached and gave her her hand and lifted her up. And both of them stood together, and the brutality of the populace being appeased, they were recalled to the Sanavivarian gate.

Then Perpetua was received by a certain one who was still a catechumen, Rusticus by name, who kept close to her and she, as if aroused from sleep, so deeply had she been in the Spirit and in an ecstasy, began to look round her and to say to the amazement of all, "I cannot tell when we are to be led out to that cow." And when she had heard what had already happened, she did not believe it until she had perceived certain signs of injury in her body and in her dress, and had recognized the catechumen. Afterwards causing that catechumen and the brother to approach, she addressed them saying, "Stand fast in the faith and love one another, all of you, and be not offended at my sufferings."

The same Saturus at the other entrance exhorted the soldier Pudens saying, "Assuredly here I am, as I have promised and foretold, for up to this moment I have felt no beast. And now believe with your whole heart. Lo, I am going forth to that beast and I shall be destroyed with one bite of the leopard."

And immediately at the conclusion of the exhibition he was thrown to the leopard, and with one bite of his he was bathed with such a quantity of blood that the people shouted out to him

I AM A CHRISTIAN

as he was returning the testimony of his second baptism, "Saved and washed, saved and washed." Manifestly he was assuredly saved who had been glorified in such a spectacle.

Then to the soldier Pudens he said, "Farewell and be mindful of my faith, and let not these things disturb but confirm you." And at the same time he asked for a little ring from his finger and returned it to him bathed in his wound, leaving to him an inherited token and the memory of his blood. And then lifeless he is cast down with the rest to be slaughtered in the usual place.

And when the populace called for them into the midst, that as the sword penetrated into their body they might make their eyes partners in the murder, they rose up of their own accord, and transferred themselves whither the people wished, but they first kissed one another, that they might consummate their martyrdom with the kiss of peace. The rest, indeed, immovable and in silence, received the sword-thrust—much more Saturus, who also had first ascended the ladder and first gave up his spirit, for he also was waiting for Perpetua. But Perpetua, that she might taste some pain, being pierced between the ribs, cried out loudly, and she herself placed the wavering right hand of the youthful gladiator to her throat. Possibly such a woman could not have been slain unless she herself had willed it, because she was feared by the impure spirit.

O most brave and blessed martyrs! O truly called and chosen unto the glory of our Lord Jesus Christ! whom whoever magnifies and honors and adores assuredly ought to read these examples for the edification of the Church, not less than the ancient ones, so that new virtues also may testify that one and the same Holy Spirit is always operating even until now, and God the Father Omnipotent, and His Son Jesus Christ our Lord, whose is the glory and infinite power for ever and ever. Amen.[6]

NOTES

1. See the Life of Septimius Severus in the *Historia Augusta* as translated into English by David Magie in the Loeb Classical Library Edition.
2. An English translation of the Letter To Scapula, as translated by S. Thelwall may be

found in *Ante-Nicene Fathers, Volume III: Latin Christianity, Its Founder, Tertullian.*

3. Joel 2:28.
4. Perpetua's vision of Dinocrates is one of the first documented explorations of the Christian theological concept of Purgatory and the efficacy of prayers for the dead.
5. The Agape, or love-feast, was an early Christian liturgical form which had aspects in common with the Eucharist, but also seemed to involve providing sustenance to the poor. See the *Catholic Encyclopedia*, 1907 edition, available at www.newadvent.org under "agape" for a detailed description.
6. This translation of *The Passion of the Holy Martyrs Perpetua and Felicitas* was rendered by R. E. Wallis and originally published in *The Ante-Nicene Fathers, Volume III: Latin Christianity, Its Founder, Tertullian.*

Chapter 8

Potamiena, Basilides and the Pupils of Origen who Became Martyrs

The great metropolis of Alexandria in Egypt was also a center of early Christian activity. From there came the remarkable 3rd century Christian teacher Origen, a voluminous writer whose name would continue to inspire and create controversy long after his death. He was the son of a martyr. His father, Leonides, was executed for being a Christian while Origen was a child. He himself was tortured during the persecution under the emperor Decius in the early 250s AD and seems to have passed to his eternal reward as a confessor shortly thereafter.

The passage below is taken from Eusebius's Ecclesiastical History written roughly a century after the events described. Most of the various martyrs mentioned in the account were pupils of Origen who perished during the reign of Septimius Severus, probably around the year AD 210. This account is notable because it is one of the earliest authentic passages that shows explicitly how the blood of the martyrs became the seed of the Church, as Tertullian famously said. In this passage, we see the courage and nobility of the slave girl Potamiena turn the heart of the soldier Basilides toward Christ, while a post-mortem vision of the same confirmed him in the faith.

✢ ✢ ✢

By giving such evidences of a philosophic life to those who saw him, he [Origen] aroused many of his pupils to similar zeal, so that prominent men even of the unbelieving heathen and men that followed learning and philosophy were led to his instruction. Some of them having received from him into the depth of their souls faith in the Divine Word became prominent in the persecution then prevailing, and some of them were seized and suffered martyrdom.

The first of these was Plutarch. As he was led to death, the man of whom we are speaking [Origen] being with him at the end of his life, came near being slain by his fellow-citizens, as if he were the cause of his death. But the providence of God preserved him at this time also.

After Plutarch, the second martyr among the pupils of Origen was Serenus, who gave through fire a proof of the faith which he had received. The third martyr from the same school was Heraclides, and after him the fourth was Hero. The former of these was as yet a catechumen, and the latter had but recently been baptized. Both of them were beheaded. After them, the fifth from the same school proclaimed as an athlete of piety was another Serenus who, it is reported, was beheaded after a long endurance of tortures. And of women, Herais died while yet a catechumen, receiving baptism by fire, as Origen himself somewhere says.[1]

Basilides may be counted the seventh of these. He led to martyrdom the celebrated Potamiena, who is still famous among the people of the country for the many things which she endured for the preservation of her chastity and virginity. For she was blooming in the perfection of her mind and her physical graces. Having suffered much for the faith of Christ, finally after tortures dreadful and terrible to speak of, she with her mother, Marcella, was put to death by fire.

They say that the judge, Aquila by name, having inflicted severe tortures upon her entire body, at last threatened to hand her over to the gladiators for bodily abuse. After a little consideration, being asked for her decision, she made a reply which was regarded as impious. Thereupon she received sentence immediately, and Basilides, one of the officers of the army, led her to death. But as the people attempted to annoy and insult her with abusive words, he drove back her insulters, showing her much pity and kindness. And perceiving the man's sympathy for her, she exhorted him to be of good courage, for she would supplicate her Lord for him after her departure and he would soon receive a reward for the kindness he had shown her.

Having said this, she nobly sustained the issue, burning pitch being poured little by little over various parts of her body from the sole of her feet to the crown of her head. Such was the conflict endured by this famous maiden.

Not long after this Basilides, being asked by his fellow-soldiers to swear for a certain reason, declared that it was not lawful for him to swear at all, for he was a Christian and he confessed this openly. At first they thought that he was jesting, but when he continued to affirm it, he was led to the judge and acknowledging his conviction before him, he was imprisoned. But the brethren in God coming to him and inquiring the reason of this sudden and remarkable resolution, he is reported to have said that Potamiena, for three days after her martyrdom, stood beside him by night and placed a crown on his head and said that she had besought the Lord for him and had obtained what she asked, and that soon she would take him with her.

Thereupon the brethren gave him the seal of the Lord; and on the next day, after giving glorious testimony for the Lord, he was beheaded. And many others in Alexandria are recorded to have accepted speedily the word of Christ in those times, for Potamiena appeared to them in their dreams and exhorted them. But let this suffice in regard to this matter.[2]

NOTES

1. The phrase, "baptism by fire" here refers to a passage in Origen's *Homily on Jeremiah* in which he says: "Who is he who is saved in another resurrection? He who needs the baptism from fire, when he comes before that fire and the fire tests him, and when that fire finds wood, hay and stubble to burn." This is a reference to 1 Corinthians 3:12 and is a very early exploration of the concept of Purgatory. See *Origen: Homilies on Jeremiah*

     and 1 Kings 28 as translated by John Clark Smith for the *Fathers of the Church* series.
2. This passage is taken from the English translation of the *Ecclesiastical History* of Eusebius, Book IV, Chapters 3, 4, and 5 as published in *A Select Library of Nicene and Post-Nicene Fathers of the Christian Church, Volume 1: Eusebius.*

Chapter 9

The Martyrs of Alexandria during the Decian Persecution

With the death of the emperor Septimius Severus in AD 211, the Roman Empire became politically unstable, suffering through a succession of weak and perverse rulers. Through this time, the Christians continued to endure sporadic outbreaks of violence. With the arrival of Alexander Severus on the imperial throne in AD 222, a respite was granted. Alexander's mother, Julia Mammæa, had been a student of Origen though neither she nor her son apparently embraced Christianity. They were, instead, syncretists who attempted to combine all religions into one.

Though Christian populations continued to experience occasional outbreaks of violence, they soon got used to living in peace within the Empire. It was a profound shock, therefore, when the emperor Decius instituted the first true empire-wide persecution. Ostensibly to reinstitute Roman pagan piety throughout the empire as a means to restoring political order, the Decian edict which was promulgated in AD 249 enjoined all citizens of the empire to offer public sacrifice to the pagan pantheon. They would then be issued a document called a libellus, certifying that they had done so. Here is an example of a libellus from this period that has survived antiquity:

> To the commissioners of the village of Alexandrou-Nesos, elected to superintend the sacrifices. From Aurelius Diogenes, son of

Satabos, of the village of Alexandrou-Nesos, aged seventy-two years, with a scar on his right eyebrow.

I have at all times offered sacrifices to the gods, and now again in accordance with the edict in your presence I have again made sacrifice and libations and partaken of the sacred offerings, and I request you certify this statement. May you prosper. I, Aurelius Diogenes, have presented this application.

I, Aurelius Syros, have witnessed your sacrifice.

The first year of the Emperor Cæsar Gaius Messius Quintus Trajanus Decius, pious and prosperous, Augustus, on the second of the month Epiphi.[1]

Obviously, a believing Christian could not do what was necessary to receive such a certificate. As a result, a ferocious persecution erupted. For an account of the outbreak of these fresh outrages, we return to Alexandria and read an amazing letter from Saint Dionysius, patriarch of Alexandria, to his colleague, Bishop Fabian of Antioch. This epistle was preserved for posterity by Eusebius in his Ecclesiastical History. *In this, we see for the first time how many Christians who had enjoyed relative safety for so long were quick to apostasize when mortal danger threatened. At the same time, the courage of the martyrs during a time when so many of their brethren are falling away becomes that much more heroic.*

FROM AN EPISTLE FROM SAINT DIONYSIUS TO FABIAN, BISHOP OF ANTIOCH

The persecution did not begin amongst us with the Imperial edict, for it anticipated that by a whole year. And the prophet and poet of evil to this city, whoever he was, was beforehand in moving and exciting the heathen crowds against us, rekindling their zeal for the national superstitions. So they being aroused by him and availing themselves of all lawful authority for their unholy doings conceived that the only piety, the proper worship of their gods was this—to thirst for our blood.

First, then they carried off an old man, Metras, and bade him utter impious words, and when he refused they beat his body with sticks and stabbed his face and eyes with sharp bulrushes as they led him into the outskirts of the city and there stoned him.

Then they led a believer named Quinta to the idol-house and tried to make her kneel down, and when she turned away in disgust, they bound her by the feet and hauled her right through the city over the rough pavement, the big stones bruising her poor body, and at the same time beat her till they reached the same spot, and there stoned her.

Thereupon they all with one consent made a rush on the houses of the believers, and falling each upon those whom they recognized as neighbors, plundered, harried and despoiled them, setting aside the more valuable of their possessions and casting out into the streets and burning the cheaper things and such as were made of wood, till they produced the appearance of a city devastated by the enemy. But the brethren gave way and submitted and accepted the plundering of their possessions with joy like unto those of whom Paul also testified. And I know not if any, save possibly a single one who fell into their hands, up till now has denied the Lord.

Another notable case was that of the aged virgin Apollonia, whom they seized and knocked out all her teeth, striking her on the jaws. Then they made a pyre before the city and threatened to burn her alive if she would not join them in uttering blasphemies. But she asked for a brief respite, and being let go, suddenly leapt into the fire and was devoured by the flames.

Sarapion, also, they caught in his own house and after outraging him with cruel tortures and crushing all his limbs, they cast him headlong from the upper story. And we could go by no high road, thoroughfare, or byway, either by day or by night, for everywhere and always there was a constant cry that any one who did not utter words of blasphemy must be dragged off and burnt. And this state of things prevailed for some time, till the revolution and civil war occupied the attention of these unhappy men and turned on one another their fury against us. And so we had a short breathing space, as they found no leisure for raging against us. But very soon the overthrow of the ruler who had been not unfavorable to us is announced, and our grave fears of being attacked are renewed. And, in fact, the edict arrived, which was itself almost to be compared with that foretold by the Lord, well-nigh the most terrible of all, so as to cause, if possible, even the elect to stumble.

Nevertheless all were panic-stricken, and numbers at once of those who were in higher positions, some came forward in fear, and some who held public posts were led by their official duties. Others, again, were brought in by those about them and when their names were called, approached the impure and unholy sacrifices, pale and trembling in some cases as if they were not going to sacrifice but themselves become sacrifices and victims to the idols, so that they incurred ridicule from the large crowd that stood by and proved themselves to be utter cowards both in regard to death and in regard to sacrificing, whilst others ran readily up to the altar, making it plain by their forwardness that they had not been Christians even before. About such the Lord's prediction is most true that with difficulty shall they be saved. And of the rest some followed one or other of the above, while others fled or were captured. And of these last, again, some after going as far as chains and imprisonment and even after being immured several days in certain cases, still, before coming into court, forswore themselves. And others, even after enduring some amount of torment, failed at the last.

But the steadfast and blessed pillars of the Lord, being strengthened by Him and receiving due and proportionate power and endurance for the mighty Faith that was in them, proved themselves admirable witnesses of His Kingdom. Foremost among them was Julian, a sufferer from gout, unable to stand or walk. He was brought up with two others who carried him, of whom the one straightway denied the Faith. The other, Cronion by name, but surnamed Eunous (well-disposed) and the

The Martyrs of Alexandria during the Decian Persecution

old man Julian himself confessed the Lord and were conveyed on camel's back and scourged as they rode right through the city—big though it be, as ye know—and at last were burnt with fire unquenchable, whilst all the people stood round. And a soldier who stood by as they were carried along and protested against those who insulted them was denounced and brought up, to wit God's brave warrior Besas, and after heroic conduct in the great war of piety, was beheaded.

And yet another, a Libyan by race, who rightly and happily was named Mauar (happy), though the judge urged him strongly to renounce the Faith, would not give in and so was burnt alive.

After them Epimachus and Alexander, when they had remained a long time in bonds and had endured endless tortures from the "claws" and scourges, were also consumed with fire unquenchable. And with them four women: Ammonarion, a holy virgin, though the judge tortured her vigorously for a long time because she had declared beforehand that she would say nothing that he bade her, kept true to her promise and was led off to punishment. And of the rest there was the aged and reverend Mercuria and Dionysia who, though she had many children, did not love them above the Lord. These the Prefect was ashamed to go on torturing in vain and be beaten by women, and so they died by the sword without further tortures, for the brave Ammonarion had exhausted all their devices.

Then were delivered up three Egyptians: Heron, Ater and Isidore, and with them Dioscorus, a lad of about fifteen. And first of all the Prefect tried to cajole the stripling with words, thinking he could easily be won over, and then to force him by torments, thinking he would soon give in. But Dioscorus was neither persuaded nor forced. So the others he cruelly lacerated and when they too stood firm, handed them over to the fire. But Dioscorus, who had distinguished himself in public and had answered his private questionings most wisely, he let off saying that he granted him a reprieve for repenting on account of his age. And now the godly Dioscorus is still with us, having waited for his longer trial and his more determined conflict.

I AM A CHRISTIAN

Another Egyptian, Nemesion, was falsely accused of being an associate of brigands, but being accused of that most untrue charge before the centurion, he was then denounced as a Christian and came in chains before the Prefect. And he having most unjustly maltreated him with twice as many tortures and stripes as the brigands had received, burnt him to death between them, being honored, happy man, by the example of Christ.

Again a whole quaternion of soldiers—Ammon, Zenon, Ptolemy and Ingenuus, and an old man, Theophilus, with them were standing before the judgment seat whilst someone was being tried for being a Christian, and when he showed signs of denying the Faith they were so provoked as they stood by, nodding their heads and stretching out their hands and making gestures with their bodies, that they drew the general attention to themselves. And then, before any could seize them, they leapt upon the stand of their own accord saying they were Christians, so that the Prefect and his assessors were frightened, and those who were being judged seemed to take courage over what awaited them and their judges lost heart. So these soldiers walked in brave procession from the court and rejoiced in their witness (martyrdom), God giving them a glorious triumph.

And many others in the cities and villages were torn asunder by the heathen (Gentiles), one of which I will mention as an example. Ischyrion acted as steward to one of the authorities at a wage. His employer bade him sacrifice, ill-treated him when he refused, and on his persistence drove him forth with insults. When he still stood his ground, he took a big stick and killed him by driving it through his vital parts.

What need to mention the multitude of those who wandered in deserts and mountains consumed by hunger and thirst and cold and diseases and brigands and wild beasts, the survivors of whom bear witness to their election and victory? Of these, also, I will bring forward one instance by way of illustration. Chæremon was the aged Bishop of what is called Nilopolis. He fled to the Arabian hills with his wife and never returned, nor were they ever seen again by the brethren who made long search, but found neither them nor their bodies. And there were many who on those very Arabian hills were sold into slavery by the barbarian Saracens, of whom some were with difficulty ransomed at high sums, and others even yet have not been ransomed. And these things I have described at length, brother, not without purpose, but in order that thou mightest know how many terrible things have taken place amongst us, of which those who have had more experience will know of more cases than I do.[2]

NOTES

1. This sample libellus was taken from the article: "A Light on the Early Persecutions," by A. Hilliard Atteridge, in *America: A Catholic Review of the Week*, July 6, 1918.
2. This passage is taken from an epistle of Saint Dionysius to Fabian, bishop of Antioch as recorded in the *Ecclesiastical History* of Eusebius, Book VI, Chapters 41 and 42. The English translation originally appeared in *A Select Library of Nicene and Post-Nicene Fathers of the Christian Church, Volume I: Eusebius.*

Chapter 10

The Passion of Saint Saturninus

The Decian persecution impacted the length and breadth of the Roman Empire for the period of about two years. From Alexandria, we next turn our attention 1,500 miles northwest to Gaul—modern day France. The text that follows is one of the most ancient authentic Christian documents from that Roman province to survive antiquity.

The Passion of Saturninus was compiled in its present form in the early 5th century AD upon the transfer of the saint's remains to a new basilica built by Saint Exuperius, bishop of Toulouse. The story of the transfer along with the introduction and conclusion flow clearly from the pen of a later writer. The core martyrdom account, however, is considerably older. We know from Gregory of Tours's *History of the Franks, that Saturninus was one of the seven bishops sent, most likely by Pope Fabian, to preach the Gospel in Gaul during the consulship of Decius and Gratus—that is, AD 250. It is not known for certain whether his martyrdom occurred immediately after his arrival during the reign of Decius, or during the subsequent persecution under Valerian in AD 258.

This translation of the Passion in English was commissioned by Roger Pearse, the indefatigable editor at the Tertullian.org website, and rendered by Andrew Eastbourne. Messrs. Pearse and Eastbourne are very generous in putting this valuable work in the public domain.

I AM A CHRISTIAN

On the Passion and Translation of Saint Saturninus, Bishop of the City of Toulouse, and Martyr

We revere with due admiration the most blessed sufferings of those who, as we have heard and believe (through the good service of the fame that reports the information), have been sanctified by a happy martyrdom. We honor with vigils, hymns and even solemn sacraments those days on which they were crowned with [God's] gift after victory, striving as they bore witness to the name of the Lord, and by their blessed death being reborn in the heavenly realms of the same Lord, who helped them with his own power in their struggle—[and we do this] so that we may ask for their protection and support before the Lord by praying and deserve it by honoring [them]. With what solemnity, then, shall we revere, with what joy shall we observe that day, on which the most blessed Saturninus, bishop of the city of Toulouse and martyr, earned in that same city a double crown (as God is my witness)—the rank of bishop and the honor of martyrdom—so that his suffering sanctified one whose life had already made him worthy of reverence!

At that time (after the bodily coming of the Savior) the true Sun of Righteousness had risen in the darkness and had begun to illuminate the Western districts—for gradually, little by little, the sound of the Gospels went out into the whole world, and the preaching of the Apostles in its slow advance shone forth in our regions. A few churches were being built in some cities, through the devotion of a small number of Christians, while numerous temples in all places were sending up the disgusting smoke [of sacrifices], through the lamentable error of the pagans.

Then (truly quite a long time ago, that is, during the consulship of Decius and Gratus, as the faithful report tells), the city of Toulouse had received Saturninus as its first and supreme priest of Christ. By his faith and virtue, the oracles of those demons who were worshipped in this same city began to cease. Their fabrications were laid bare, their machinations uncovered, all their power among the pagans, all their deceit, began to decrease as the faith of the Christians increased. Since the aforementioned bishop in his going to and from the church which was quite small at that time, often went past the Capitol, which was between his house and the house of God, the deceitful crowd of demons was not able to stand the holy man's presence, and the statues (mute as they were), overshadowed by no apparitions, remained in silence [as their only response] to the impious worship and the customary prayers of those who came to consult them.

All the priests of impious superstition, disturbed by the novelty of such a great thing, began to ask themselves whence this muteness (not usual for such a long time) had suddenly come upon their gods, and who had shut their ever-babbling mouths so that they, not moved by the prayers of those who called upon them nor charmed by the shed blood of bulls and so many sacrifices, refused to give any response to those who consulted them—[were they] angry or absent? They heard from a certain enemy of our religion that some sect hostile to pagan superstition had arisen which was called Christian, and that it was striving to destroy their gods. Also, the bishop of this faith was Saturninus, who passed by the Capitol frequently. It was at the sight of this man that the mouths of their gods were terrified and fell silent. They could not easily be re-opened unless an accelerated death took that bishop away.

O unhappy error and blind madness! They heard that the man was a terror to their own gods and that the demons went into exile from their temples and their habitations when he passed by. Not only did they hear—they also understood! And they would prefer to kill this man, who was terrifying to the idols they worshipped even without making any threats, rather than to honor him. Miserable people—who did not consider that they ought to worship no one more than him whose servant had given orders to their own divinities! For what is more foolish than to fear those who are afraid and not to fear that one who rules over the rulers?

In the midst of this eager questioning and astonishment, as little by little a great multitude of people had gathered and they

I AM A CHRISTIAN

were all eagerly wanting to find out something certain regarding all this talk, and (a bull having been prepared as a victim) they were desiring either to bring their gods back or propitiate them by the sacrifice of such a tremendous victim—see! the holy Saturninus himself, coming to a solemn service, was recognized by one of that malicious crowd who said, "Look! The adversary of our worship himself, the standard-bearer of the new religion, who preaches the destruction of temples, who despises our gods by calling them demons, whose constant presence, finally, prevents us from obtaining oracles! And so, since the end he deserves has presented the very man to us at the opportune time, let us take vengeance for the injury to ourselves and to our gods at the same time! And now, through our compulsion, may he either be pleasing to them by sacrificing, or make them joyful by dying!"

With the urging of such an impious voice, the whole crowd of lunatics surrounded the holy man and, once a priest and two deacons who had accompanied him had fallen away in flight, he was brought alone to the Capitol. As they were trying to force him to sacrifice to the demons, he bore witness in a clear voice: "I know only one God, the true God. I will offer to Him the sacrifice of praise. I know that your gods are demons, and you honor them (in vain) not so much by the sacrifice of cattle as by the deaths of your own souls. Now, how is it that you want me to fear those by whom, as I hear, you say I am feared?"

At these words of the holy bishop, the whole boisterous, impious multitude was inflamed and used that bull which had been prepared as a sacrificial victim in the service of their savagery, tying a rope around its flanks and leaving it loose in back. They bound the holy man's feet with the end of the rope that was hanging down behind the bull and drove the bull with rather sharp blows to rush down from the upper part of the Capitol onto the plain. Without delay, during the first part of the descent of that slope, his head having been dashed [against the rocks], his brain having been scattered, and his body having been mangled in every part, his soul, worthy of God, was received by

Christ so that after the victory He [i.e., Christ] might crown with His own laurels [the soul] that pagan fury had wrenched out with torments while he was fighting faithfully for Christ's name.

The dead body, however, now exposed to no one's affronts, was led by the bull in its frenzy to that place where, the rope having snapped in two, it received burial in a mound at that time. For since at that time the Christians themselves were afraid to bury the body of the holy man on account of the pagans' agitation, only two women, overcoming the weakness of their sex by the power of their faith, braver than all the men, and encouraged by the example of their bishop, I believe, to endure martyrdom, put the body of the blessed man into a wooden coffin and, after making deep trenches, placed it as far underground as possible. And so, they seemed not so much to be burying the sacred remains (so worthy of reverence in their eyes) as to be hiding them for fear that people of impious mind, perchance, if they saw any honors being paid to the buried body's grave, might immediately dig up the body and tear it to pieces, and even take away the modest tomb. But the Lord took up his martyr in peace—to Him belong honor and glory, power and might for ever and ever. Amen.

The body of the martyr remained for a certain amount of time under the common turf, not honored by any [human being] but honored by God—until Saint Hilarius, ordained bishop in the city of Toulouse much later, learned about the death and merit of his predecessor, had the earth dug up as far as the wooden coffin itself. Since he was afraid to move the holy remains, he carefully had a vault built above it with many bricks, and to a place of prayer of the same size, he added a quite small basilica made of ordinary timber—keeping the body hidden, of course, so that faithless people would not dig it up and rip it apart.

As time wore on, the remains of many people who were departing from the world were faithfully brought to this little basilica for comfort on account of the body of the martyr resting there. And the whole place was filled with a great number of interred bodies. Then the bishop, Saint Silvius, who had attained the episcopacy of the aforementioned city, was preparing a beautiful and fine-looking basilica at great cost in order to transfer the remains of the venerable martyr there—but he departed from the world before the completion of the work he had begun.

After his death, Saint Exuperius, who had been elected into the highest priesthood—a man entirely free of [the desire to do] harm to any of his forebears, entirely free of envy towards any of those who were seen to be ruling the churches at that time, not only second to none, but even worthy of comparison with the blessed martyr himself in the merits of his virtues—most industriously completed the basilica that his predecessor had faithfully begun, and auspiciously dedicated it.

While he was hesitating to transfer the remains of the holy martyr there—not for any disbelief of his own, but for the honor of that man himself—he was admonished in a dream not to neglect faithlessly what he had believed faithfully: no injury was done to spirits either by the diminution of their ashes or the transportation of their bodies, since it was a manifest fact that what had fostered the salvation of believers was [also] conducive to the honor of martyrs. Straightway, bolstered by such a vision, he sent a request to the pious emperors and without any delay, attained what he had asked so devoutly, so that the remains of the holy man, [now] transferred to the basilica that had been prepared with all zeal, would not be violated by reckless audacity, but rather honored by the deference of one who showed quite attentive reverence.

Now as to what remains for this little work: let all who read it, let all who hear it, understand that the source of our salvation stands in faith, and that the Lord did not without reason say in the words of the Gospel: "Do you believe this?"—and when the answer was given, "I believe," He said: "Let it be done for you according to your faith"[1]—not because the Lord, who examines the heart and mind, was ignorant of that their state of belief, but in order to remind us not to believe doubtfully what is said about the Lord's virtues, or [believe doubtfully] in what we ask to be granted to us.

For this reason the Savior himself said about such men: "If you carry out my will, I shall no longer call you servants but friends."[2] And the same [Savior] bore witness through the voice of the prophet: "To me, however, your friends are greatly honored, O God,"[3] and again: "These are the ones who have come out of the great tribulation, who have washed their robes in the blood of the Lamb, who follow the Lamb"[4]—about their blessedness it was said: "Planted in the house of the Lord, they flourished in the courts of our God,"[5] and again: "Precious in the sight of the Lord is the death of his saints,"[6] and again: "The saints will exult in glory, they will rejoice in their beds,"[7] and again: "This glory belongs to all his saints."[8] To them it was granted not only to believe in Christ, but also to suffer for Christ and be with Christ immediately after the dissolution of their bodies.

Let us not neglect the friends of God and the well-beloved of God as being dead. Rather, let us honor them as living—for it is certain by indubitable faith that if we should faithfully request their favor, we shall happily feel their support, because even if their enthusiasm ceased, He would supply our desires, [He] who not only examines present thoughts, but also knows future thoughts. When requests are made to Him in His own [people], He understands that He [Himself] is being honored.

Under the reign of our Lord Jesus Christ, to whom belong honor and glory forever and ever. Amen.[9]

NOTES

1. Matthew 9:28-29.
2. John 15:15.
3. Psalms 138:17.
4. Apocalypse 7:14.
5. Psalms 91:14.
6. Psalms 115:15.
7. Psalms 149:5.
8. Psalms 149:9.
9. This English translation of the *Passion of Saint Saturninus* was rendered by Andrew Eastbourne and first published on the tremendously useful website, Tertullian.org. Permission for re-use in print was granted by Roger Pearse who maintains the aforementioned site.

Chapter 11

The Martyrdom of Saint Cyprian

At the Battle of Abritus in AD 251, the emperor Decius was utterly defeated and killed by the Goths. The Christian scholar Lactantius, writing about 50 years later, reports that Decius, "was suddenly surrounded by the barbarians and slain, together with a great part of his army. Nor could he be honored with the rites of sepulture, but stripped and naked, he lay to be devoured by wild beasts and birds—a fit end for the enemy of God."[1]

Following this disgraceful death, the persecution instigated by Decius also petered out for a few years while the empire dealt with numerous internal uprisings and foreign invasions. The situation was still very unstable when Valerian took the imperial throne in AD 253. While engaged in fighting with the Persians on the eastern frontier in AD 257, Valerian commenced a new empire-wide persecution. His rationale was very similar to that of Decius. He issued a very severe imperial rescript commanding that Christian bishops and priests be summarily executed, that Christian men of high rank be degraded, stripped of their wealth and, if they persisted in their Christianity, subjected to capital punishment.

Bishops across the empire were slain during the persecution of Valerian, including Pope Sixtus II. Perhaps the most famous prelate martyred during this persecution, however, was Thaschus Cæcilius Cyprianus, Bishop of Carthage. Known to posterity as Saint Cyprian, his name appears to this day in the canon of the Catholic Mass. He was one of the outstanding Christian writers and apologists of the early Church and much of his work has come down to us from antiquity. Cyprian had escaped the persecution of Decius by going into hiding—an action for which he was criticized unjustly by some of his contemporaries. During the persecution of Valerian, however, he was captured.

We are indebted to Pontius, one of Cyprian's deacons, for the following eye-witness account of his martyrdom. It is part of a more complete Life which we have excerpted for our purposes here. To read the full ancient biography, see The Complete Works of Saint Cyprian of Carthage which is available as part of the Christian Roman Empire series. These excerpts pick up the story at the time of Cyprian's capture.

Along with Pontius's testimony, we have interspersed passages from the Acta Proconsularia Cypriani, a transcript of Saint Cyprian's trials before the proconsuls Paternus and Galerius. These excerpts provide additional detail to this fascinating account.

EXCERPTED FROM THE *ACTA PROCONSULARIA CYPRIANI*

In the fourth consulship of the emperor Valerian and the third of Gallienus, on the third before the Kalends of September, in the council chamber of Carthage, Paternus, the proconsul, said to Bishop Cyprian: "The most sacred emperors, Valerian and Gallienus have thought fit to give me a letter according to which they have ordered that those who do not practice the Roman religion should recognize the Roman rites. I have asked, therefore, concerning your name. What do you answer me?"

Bishop Cyprian said: "I am a Christian and a bishop. I have known no other gods except the true and only God, who made heaven and earth, the sea and all that is in them. To this God we Christians yield ourselves. To Him we pray by day and night for you, for all men, and for the safety of the emperors themselves."

Paternus, the proconsul, said: "Do you, then, persist in this purpose?"

Bishop Cyprian replied: "A good purpose, which has known God, cannot be changed."

The Martyrdom of Saint Cyprian

Paternus, the proconsul, said: "Will you be able to depart into exile, then, to the city of Curubitana (Curubis) according to the decree of Valerian and Gallienus?"

Bishop Cyprian said: "I depart."

Paternus, the proconsul, said: "They have thought fit to write to me not only concerning bishops, but also presbyters. I wish, therefore, to learn from you who the presbyters are who abide in the city."

Bishop Cyprian replied: "By your laws you have rightfully and profitably decreed that there should be no informers, and hence they cannot be betrayed and denounced by me. But in their own cities they will be found."

Paternus, the proconsul, said: "Today, in this place, I am going to seek them."

Cyprian said: "Since custom forbids that any one offer himself voluntarily, and this is displeasing to your judgment, they cannot give themselves up, but if you seek them, you will find them."

Paternus, the proconsul, said: "They will be found by me." And added: "It has also been ordered that they should not hold assemblies in any place or enter the cemeteries. If any one does not observe this so wholesome ordinance he is to be beheaded."

Bishop Cyprian replied: "Do as you are ordered."

Then Paternus, the proconsul, ordered the blessed bishop Cyprian to be led into exile. When he had remained there for a long time, the proconsul Galerius Maximus succeeded the proconsul Aspasius Paternus and ordered the holy bishop Cyprian to be recalled from exile and brought before him. When the holy martyr Cyprian, chosen by God, had returned from the city of Curubitana where he had been sent into exile by the order of Aspasius Paternus, the proconsul at that time, he remained in his gardens according to holy injunction, and thence daily hoped that it would happen to him as had been revealed.

While he was waiting here, there suddenly came to him on the Ides of September in the consulship of Tuscus and Bassus, two men of high rank: one the curator of the official Galerius Maximus, the proconsul, who had succeeded Aspasius Paternus, and the other the groom from the guards of this same official. And they put him between them and brought him to Sexti, where Galerius Maximus, the proconsul, had retired for the sake of recovering his health. And so the proconsul Galerius Maximus ordered Cyprian to be reserved for him until the next day. And at the same time the blessed Cyprian retired, led away to the chief and curator of this same official, Galerius Maximus, the proconsul, a most illustrious man, and he stayed with this man, enjoying his hospitality in the village called Saturui, which is between Venerea and Salutaria. Thither the whole company of brethren came and, when the holy Cyprian learned this, he ordered the maidens to be protected, since all had remained in the village before the gate of the hospitable officer.

Excerpted from *The Life and Passion of Cyprian* by Pontius the Deacon

At the bidding of the proconsul, the officer with his soldiers on a sudden came unexpectedly on him—or rather to speak more truly thought that he had come unexpectedly on him at his gardens—at his gardens, I say, which at the beginning of his faith he had sold, and which, being restored by God's mercy, he would assuredly have sold again for the use of the poor if he had not wished to avoid ill-will from the persecutors. But when could a mind ever prepared be taken unawares as if by an unforeseen attack? Therefore now he went forward, certain that what had been long delayed would be settled.

    He went forward with a lofty and elevated mien, manifesting cheerfulness in his look and courage in his heart. But being delayed to the morrow, he returned from the prætorium to the officer's house, when on a sudden a scattered rumor prevailed throughout all Carthage that now Thascius [Cyprian] was brought forward, whom there was nobody who did not know as well for his illustrious fame in the honorable opinion of all, as on account of the recollection of his most renowned work. On all sides all men were flocking together to a spectacle, to us glorious from the devotion of faith, and to be mourned over even by the Gentiles. A gentle custody, however, had him in charge when taken and placed for one night in the officer's house, so that we, his associates and friends, were as usual in his company. The whole people in the meantime, in anxiety that nothing should be done throughout the night without their knowledge, kept watch before the officer's door. The goodness of God granted him at that time, so truly worthy of it, that even God's people should watch on the passion of the priest. Yet, perhaps, some one may ask what was the reason of his returning from the prætorium to the officer. And some think that this arose from the fact, that for his own part the proconsul was then unwilling. Far be it from me to complain in matters divinely ordered of slothfulness or aversion in the proconsul. Far be it from me to admit such an evil into the consciousness of a religious mind, as that the fancy of man should decide the fate of so blessed a martyr. But the morrow, which a year before the divine condescension had foretold, required to be literally the morrow.

At last that other day dawned—that destined, that promised, that divine day—which, if even the tyrant himself had wished to put off, he would not have had any power to do so; the day rejoicing at the consciousness of the future martyr; and the clouds being scattered throughout the circuit of the world, the day shone upon them with a brilliant sun. He went out from the house of the officer, though he was the officer of Christ and God, and was walled in on all sides by the ranks of a mingled multitude. And such a numberless army hung upon his company, as if they had come with an assembled troop to assault death itself.

Now as he went, he had to pass by the race-course. And rightly, and as if it had been contrived on purpose, he had to pass by the place of a corresponding struggle who, having finished his contest, was running to the crown of righteousness. But when he had come to the prætorium, as the proconsul had not yet come forth, a place of retirement was accorded him. There, as he sat moistened after his long journey with excessive perspiration (the seat was by chance covered with linen, so that even in the very moment of his passion he might enjoy the honor of the episcopate), one of the officers ("Tesserarius") who had formerly been a Christian, offered him his clothes, as if he might wish to change his moistened garments for drier ones. And he doubtless coveted nothing further in respect of his proffered kindness than to possess the now blood-stained sweat of the martyr going to God.

He made reply to him and said, "We apply medicines to annoyances which probably today will no longer exist." Is it any wonder that he despised suffering in body who had despised death in soul? Why should we say more?

He was suddenly announced to the proconsul. He is brought forward. He is placed before him. He is interrogated as to his name. He answers who he is, and nothing more.

CONTINUED FROM THE *ACTA PROCONSULARIA CYPRIANI*

And thus on the next day, the eighteenth before the Kalends of October, early in the morning, a great crowd came to Sexti according to the order of Galerius Maximus, the proconsul. And accordingly Galerius Maximus the proconsul ordered Cyprian to be brought before him that day while he was sitting in the Sauciolian court.

And when he had been brought, Galerius Maximus, the proconsul, said to bishop Cyprian: "You are Thascius Cyprian?"

Bishop Cyprian replied: "I am."

Galerius Maximus, the proconsul, said: "The most sacred emperors have commanded you to sacrifice."

Bishop Cyprian said: "I will not."

Galerius Maximus said: "Reflect on it."

Bishop Cyprian replied: "Do what you are ordered to do. In such a just case there is no need of reflection."

Galerius Maximus, having spoken with the council, pronounced the sentence weakly and reluctantly in the following words: "For a long time you have lived in sacrilege, you have gathered about you many associates in your impious conspiracy, you have put yourself in hostility to the Roman gods and to the

The Martyrdom of Saint Cyprian

sacred rites, nor could the pious and most sacred princes, Valerian and Gallienus, emperors, and Valerian, the most noble Cæsar, bring you back to the practice of their worship. And therefore, since you are found to be the author of the vilest crimes and the standard bearer, you shall be a warning to those whom you have gathered about you in your crime. By your blood, discipline shall be established."

And having said this he read out the decree from his tablet: "We command that Thascius Cyprian be executed by the sword."

Bishop Cyprian said: "Thank God."

After this sentence the crowd of brethren kept saying: "And we will be beheaded with him." On account of this, a commotion arose among the brethren and a great crowd followed him.

Continued from *The Life and Passion of Cyprian*, by Pontius the Deacon

And thus, therefore, the judge reads from his tablet the sentence which lately in the vision he had not read—a spiritual sentence, not rashly to be spoken—a sentence worthy of such a bishop and such a witness, a glorious sentence wherein he was called a standard bearer of the sect, and an enemy of the gods, and one who was to be an example to his people, and that with his blood discipline would begin to be established. Nothing could be more complete, nothing more true, than this sentence. For all the things which were said, although said by a heathen, are divine.

Nor is it indeed to be wondered at since priests are accustomed to prophesy of the passion. He had been a standard bearer, who was accustomed to teach concerning the bearing of Christ's standard. He had been an enemy of the gods, who commanded the idols to be destroyed. Moreover, he gave example to his friends since, when many were about to follow in a similar manner, he was the first in the province to consecrate the first-fruits of martyrdom. And by his blood discipline began to be established, but it was the discipline of martyrs who, emulating their teacher in the imitation of a glory like his own, themselves also gave a confirmation to discipline by the very blood of their own example.

And when he left the doors of the prætorium, a crowd of soldiery accompanied him. And that nothing might be wanting in his passion, centurions and tribunes guarded his side. Now the place itself where he was about to suffer is level, so that it affords a noble spectacle, with its trees thickly planted on all sides. But as, by the extent of the space beyond, the view was not attainable to the confused crowd, persons who favored him had climbed up into the branches of the trees, that there might not even be wanting to him (what happened in the case of Zacchæus), that he was gazed upon from the trees. And now, having with his own hands bound his eyes, he tried to hasten the slowness of the executioner, whose office was to wield the sword, and who with difficulty clasped the blade in his failing right hand with trembling fingers, until the mature hour of glorification strengthened the hand of the centurion with power granted from above to accomplish the death of the excellent man, and at length supplied him with the permitted strength.

O blessed people of the Church, who as well in sight as in feeling, and what is more, in outspoken words, suffered with such a bishop as theirs. And, as they had ever heard him in his own discourses, were crowned by God the Judge! For although that which the general wish desired could not occur, *viz.* that the entire congregation should suffer at once in the fellowship of a like glory, yet whoever under the eyes of Christ beholding, and in the hearing of the priest, eagerly desired to suffer, by the sufficient testimony of that desire did in some sort send a missive to God, as his ambassador.

His passion being thus accomplished, it resulted that Cyprian, who had been an example to all good men, was also the first who in Africa imbued his priestly crown with blood of martyrdom, because he was the first who began to be such after the apostles. For from the time at which the episcopal order is enumerated at Carthage, not one is ever recorded, even of good men and priests, to have come to suffering, although devotion surrendered to God is always in consecrated men reckoned instead of martyrdom. Yet Cyprian attained even to the perfect crown by the consummation of the Lord, so that in that very city in which he had in such wise lived, and in which he had been the first to do many noble deeds, he also was the first to decorate the insignia of his heavenly priesthood with glorious gore.

What shall I do now? Between joy at his passion and grief at still remaining, my mind is divided in different directions, and twofold affections are burdening a heart too limited for them. Shall I grieve that I was not his associate? But yet I must triumph in his victory. Shall I triumph at his victory? Still I grieve that I am not his companion. Yet still to you I must in simplicity confess, what you also are aware of, that it was my intention to be his companion. Much and excessively I exult at his glory, but still more do I grieve that I remained behind.[2]

The conclusion from the *Acta Proconsularia Cypriani*

And thus Cyprian was brought to the country about Sexti. Here he laid aside his red cloak, kneeled on the ground, and prostrated himself before the Lord in prayer. And when he had laid aside his priestly robe and given it to the deacons, he stood in his linen under-garments, and waited for the executioner. Moreover, when the executioner had come, he ordered his followers to give this executioner twenty-five pieces of gold. Indeed linen cloths and handkerchiefs were being sent before him by the brethren.

After this the blessed Cyprian covered his eyes with his hand. When he could not bind the handkerchiefs to himself, Julian the presbyter, and Julian the subdeacon, bound them. Thus the blessed Cyprian died, and his body was placed near at hand on account of the curiosity of the heathen. Hence, being borne away in the night with tapers and torches, it was brought with prayers and great triumph to the courts of the procurator Macrobius Candidianus, which are on the Via Mappaliensis, near the fish ponds.

I AM A CHRISTIAN

Moreover, after a few days, Galerius Maximus, the proconsul, died.³

NOTES

1. This quote is taken from Lactantius's work, *Of the Manner in Which the Persecutors Died*, translated into English by William Fletcher and originally published in *The Ante-Nicene Christian Library, Volume 12: The Works of Lactantius, Volume 2*.
2. The excerpts from the *Life and Passion of Cyprian, Bishop and Martyr*, are taken from *The Complete Works of Saint Cyprian* edited by Phillip Campbell.
3. The excerpts from the *Acta Proconsularia Cypriani* are taken from *Translations and Reprints from the Original Sources of European History, Volume IV*.

CHAPTER 12

The Martyrdom of Saint Lawrence

Saint Lawrence (Laurentius) was a deacon of the Roman Church who was executed for professing Christ during the persecution of the Valerian in AD 258. His death followed a few days after the martyrdoms of Pope Sixtus II (see epitaph by Pope Damasus on page 179) and the other six deacons of Rome, Lawrence being the last to be captured. He was buried in the cemetery of Saint Cyriaca, where the present-day church of Saint Lawrence Outside the Walls now stands. Lawrence became one of the most celebrated martyrs of the early Church, and is commemorated by name in the traditional Canon of the Roman Catholic Mass.

The first notice provided here is a very brief epitaph recorded by Pope Damasus in the late 4th century which relates the martyr's sufferings in broad terms. The second passage is taken from a homily of Saint Ambrose of Milan, given about 130 years after the death of Lawrence. Entitled On the Duties of the Clergy, it shows the key aspects of Lawrence's story (his handing over the treasures of the Church, and his death on a gridiron) were known in the late 4th century. The dialogue between Lawrence and Sixtus may have been embellished by Saint Ambrose.

The third passage is an early description of his martyrdom taken from a homily given by Pope Saint Leo the Great on the occasion of Saint Lawrence's feast day (August 10) in the mid-5th century AD. The similarities between this text and Saint Ambrose's account, written about 70 years prior, are evident.

Epitaph of Pope Damasus on the Martyr, Saint Lawrence

The faith of Lawrence alone could vanquish the butcher's stripes, flames, torments and chains. Damasus, a suppliant, piles these altars with gifts, having regard to the exceeding merit of the martyr.[1]

Excerpts from *On the Duties of the Clergy* by Saint Ambrose

Let us not pass by Saint Lawrence who, seeing Sixtus his bishop led to martyrdom, began to weep, not at his sufferings but at the fact that he himself was to remain behind. With these words he began to address him:

"Where, father, are you going without your son? Where, holy priest, are you hastening without your deacon? Never were you wont to offer sacrifice without an attendant. What are you displeased at in me, my father? Have you found me unworthy? Prove, then, whether you have chosen a fitting servant. To him to whom you have entrusted the consecration of the Savior's blood, to whom you have granted fellowship in partaking of the Sacraments, to him do you refuse a part in your death? Beware lest your good judgment be endangered, while your fortitude receives its praise. The rejection of a pupil is the loss of the teacher. Or how is it that noble and illustrious men gain the victory in the contests of their scholars rather than in their own? Abraham offered his son. Peter sent Stephen on before him! Father, show forth your courage in your son. Offer me whom you have trained, that you, confident in your choice of me, may reach the crown in worthy company.

Then Sixtus said: "I leave you not nor forsake you. Greater struggles yet await you. We as old men have to undergo an easier fight—a more glorious triumph over the tyrant awaits you, a young man. Soon shall you come. Cease weeping. After three days you shall follow me. This interval must come between the priest and his levite. It was not for you to conquer under the eye of your master, as though you needed a helper. Why do you seek to share in my death? I leave to you its full inheritance. Why do you need my presence? Let the weak disciples go before their master, let the brave follow him, that they may conquer without him. For they no longer need his guidance. So Elijah left Elisha. To you I entrust the full succession to my own courage."

Such was their contention, and surely a worthy one, wherein priest and attendant strove as to who should be the first to suffer for the name of Christ. When that tragic piece is played, it is said there is great applause in the theater as Pylades says he is Orestes, while Orestes declares that he is really himself. The former acted as he did, that he might die for Orestes, and Orestes, that he might not allow Pylades to be slain instead of himself. But it was not right that they should live, for each of them was guilty of parricide, the one because he had committed the crime, the other because he had helped in its commission. But here there was nothing to call holy Lawrence to act thus but his love and devotion. However, after three days he was placed upon the gridiron by the tyrant whom he mocked, and was burnt. He said: "The flesh is roasted, turn it and eat." So by the courage of his mind he overcame the power of fire.[2]

After some additional admonitions against the love of money, Ambrose returns to the story of Lawrence later in the homily:

I once brought odium on myself because I broke up the sacred vessels to redeem captives.... These, then, I preferred to hand over to you as free men, rather than to store up the gold....

Such gold the holy martyr Lawrence preserved for the Lord. For when the treasures of the Church were demanded from him, he promised that he would show them. On the following day he brought the poor together. When asked where the treasures were which he had promised, he pointed to the poor, saying: "These are the treasures of the Church." And truly they were treasures, in whom Christ lives, in whom there is faith in Him.

So, too, the Apostle says: "We have this treasure in earthen vessels."[3] What greater treasures has Christ than those in whom

He says He Himself lives? For thus it is written: "I was hungry and you gave Me to eat, I was thirsty and you gave Me to drink, I was a stranger and you took Me in."[4] And again: "What you did to one of these, you did it unto Me."[5]

What better treasures has Jesus than those in which He loves to be seen? These treasures Lawrence pointed out and prevailed, for the persecutors could not take them away....Lawrence, who preferred to spend the gold of the Church on the poor rather than to keep it in hand for the persecutor, received the sacred crown of martyrdom for the unique and deep-sighted vigor of his meaning.[6]

Sermon LXXXV of Pope Saint Leo the Great on the Feast of Saint Lawrence

How gloriously strong in this most excellent manner of doctrine the blessed martyr Lawrence is, by whose sufferings today is marked, even his persecutors were able to feel, when they found that his wondrous courage, born principally of love for Christ, not only did not yield itself but also strengthened others by the example of his endurance.

For when the fury of the gentile potentates was raging against Christ's most chosen members and attacked those especially who were of priestly rank, the wicked persecutor's wrath was vented on Laurentius the deacon, who was pre-eminent not only in the performance of the sacred rites, but also in the management of the church's property, promising himself double spoil from one man's capture: for if he forced him to surrender the sacred treasures, he would also drive him out of the pale of true religion. And so this man, so greedy of money and such a foe to the truth, arms himself with double weapon: with avarice to plunder the gold, and with impiety to carry off Christ. He demands of the guileless guardian of the sanctuary that the church wealth on which his greedy mind was set should be brought to him. But the holy deacon showed him where he had them stored, by pointing to the many troops of poor saints, in the feeding and clothing of whom he had a store of riches which he could not lose, and which were the more entirely safe that the money had been spent on so holy a cause.

The baffled plunderer, therefore, frets, and blazing out into hatred of a religion which had put riches to such a use, determines to pillage a still greater treasure by carrying off that sacred deposit, wherewith he was enriched, as he could find no solid hoard of money in his possession. He orders Laurentius to renounce Christ, and prepares to ply the deacon's stout courage with frightful tortures. And, when the first elicit nothing, fiercer follow. His limbs, torn and mangled by many cutting blows, are commanded to be broiled upon the fire in an iron framework, which was of itself already hot enough to burn him, and on which his limbs were turned from time to time, to make the torment fiercer, and the death more lingering.

You gain nothing, you prevail nothing, O savage cruelty. His mortal frame is released from your devices, and, when Laurentius departs to heaven, you are vanquished. The flame of Christ's love could not be overcome by your flames, and the fire which burnt outside was less keen than that which blazed within.[7]

NOTES

1. This English translation of Damasus's epitaph of Saint Laurence is taken from *Christian Inscriptions* by H. P. V. Nunn.
2. This passage is taken from *On the Duties of the Clergy* by Saint Ambrose, Book I, Chapter 41 as translated into English by H. De Romestin in *A Select Library of Nicene and Post-Nicene Fathers of the Christian Church, Volume X: Saint Ambrose*.
3. 2 Corinthians 4:7.
4. Matthew 25:35.
5. Matthew 25:40.
6. This passage was also taken from *On the Duties of the Clergy*, Book II, Chapter 28. See note 2 above for more information.
7. This passage is taken from Homily 85 of Pope Saint Leo the Great, as translated into English by Charles Lett Feltoe in *A Select Library of Nicene and Post-Nicene Fathers of the Christian Church, Volume XII: Leo the Great, Gregory the Great*.

CHAPTER 13

The Passion of Saint Fructuosus of Tarragona and Companions

From Rome and Carthage, we now turn our attention to Spain where in the city of Tarragona, the persecution of Valerian and Gallienus found more victims. Saint Fructuosus was bishop of Tarragona, a city of great antiquity in northeastern Spain, and aside from the acts recorded in his martyrdom account, almost nothing is known of him. It is believed that the passage below was written by an eyewitness sometime shortly after the events described in the mid-3rd century.

Fructuosus and his two deacons, Augurius and Eulogius, were also the subjects of a poem by the late 4th century Spanish Latin poet, Prudentius (see Chapter 19 for more about Prudentius), and a sermon by Saint Augustine in the early 5th century, both of which closely reflect the facts presented here. That both of these writers refer to this account greatly enhances its claim to authenticity. The account evinces only minimal attempts by later Christian copyists to embellish the story and retains much of the tone of the legal transcript that likely formed the basis of it.

In the reign of Valerian and Gallienus, in the consulship of Æmilianus and Bassus, on January 16th, a Sunday, Fructuosus the bishop, Augurius and Eulogius, deacons, were arrested. Fructuosus had just gone to bed when the soldiers arrived. They

I AM A CHRISTIAN

were called Aurelius, Testucius, Ælius, Pollentius, Donatius and Maximus. The bishop, hearing the sound of their steps, jumped out of bed, and came to the threshold of the door.

The soldiers said to him: "Come. The governor has summoned you with your deacons."

Fructuosus replied: "Let us go. Will you let me put on my shoes?"

The soldiers replied: "As you like."

They took them to prison. Fructuosus exulted at the thought of the crown which was offered him. He prayed without ceasing. All the community came to see him, they brought him food and commended themselves to his remembrance. On one of the days which followed his imprisonment, he baptized a catechumen called Rogatianus. The accused remained six days in prison. The sixth day, January 21, a Friday, they appeared in court.

The governor Æmilianus said: "Bring in Fructuosus the bishop, Augurius and Eulogius the deacons."

An official answered: "They are present."

Æmilianus said to Fructuosus: "You know the orders of the emperors?"

Fructuosus answered: "No, but I am a Christian."

Æmilianus said: "They have ordered you to adore the gods."

Fructuosus: "I adore one God only, who has made heaven and earth, the sea and all things."

Æmilianus: "Do you know that there are gods?"

Fructuosus: "I know nothing of it."

Æmilianus threatened: "You will learn it."

Fructuosus raised his eyes to heaven and prayed in silence.

Æmilianus: "Who then will be obeyed, feared and honored if one refuses to worship the gods and adoration to the emperors?"

Æmilianus said to Augurius, the deacon: "Do not listen to what Fructuosus says."

Fructuosus answered: "I adore God the Almighty."

Æmilianus to Eulogius the deacon: "Do you adore Fructuosus?"

Eulogius: "I do not adore Fructuosus, but I adore the God

whom Fructuosus adores."

Æmilianus to Fructuosus: "You are a bishop?"

Fructuosus: "I am."

Æmilianus: "You have been." He ordered all three to be burnt alive.

During the passage to the amphitheater, the people showered pity upon Fructuosus for all, Christians and pagans, loved him. He was the perfect type of a bishop, such as the Holy Spirit had portrayed it by the hand of that vessel of election, the doctor of the Gentiles. The brethren who thought of the glory which awaited him, were more inclined to joy than sadness. Several among them presented to those who were to die a cup of spiced wine. "The hour for breaking fast has not yet sounded," said Fructuosus. It was ten o'clock.

The martyrs had solemnly celebrated in prison the day of the station the preceding Wednesday, and they advanced, joyous and calm, to finish the station of that day, Friday, with the martyrs and the prophets in the paradise which God had prepared for those whom He loves.[1] At the moment when they reached the amphitheater, a man rapidly approached the bishop. It was his reader, Augustalis, who with tears in his eyes, asked permission to unfasten his shoes. "Go away, my child, I will take off my shoes myself," said the martyr, tranquil, joyous and assured of obtaining the promise of the Lord.

When this was done, one of our people, Felix, took the right hand of the bishop, praying him to have remembrance of him. The old man said: "I must think of the Catholic Church spread from the East to the West."

As the moment approached when the martyr was going to meet glory, rather than suffering, in the presence of his brethren under the attentive gaze of the soldiers who could hear these words dictated by the Holy Spirit, Fructuosus said: "You will not be deprived of your shepherd. The goodness and promise of God will not fail you either now or in the future. What you see is but the misery of an hour."

Having comforted the brethren, the martyrs advanced

towards the place which was to be their salvation, grave and radiant at the moment of obtaining the fruit which the Scriptures promise. Like the three Hebrew children, they brought to mind the Trinity. In the midst of the flames the Father did not abandon them, the Son aided them and the Holy Spirit stood in the midst of the furnace. When the cords which bound their wrists were burnt, free in their movements the knelt down in the ordinary attitude of prayer, assured of their resurrection and recalling by hands outstretched the triumph of Christ. They did not cease to pray until the moment when they gave up their spirit.

Then divine miracles manifested themselves: the sky opened and two of our brethren, Babylas and Mydonius, belonging to the house of the prefect, and even the daughter of this officer, saw Fructuosus and his deacons, with brows crowned, entering into heaven while their dead bodies were still fastened to the stake. They called Æmilianus: "Come, see your condemned prisoners. See how according to their hope you have opened heaven to them." Æmilianus ran up, but he was unworthy to enjoy this sight.

The community was sorrowful, like a flock of sheep deprived of their shepherd. Uneasiness oppressed all, not that they pitied Fructuosus—on the contrary, they envied him.

At nightfall, the faithful hastened to the amphitheater. They carried with them wine to extinguish the bones half carbonized in the fire. Then each took for himself some portions of the ashes as relics. Another miracle exalted the faith of the brethren and served as a lesson to the youngest. It was needful that Fructuosus should bear witness in his death both to the resurrection of the body, and to the truth of that which he had promised in our Lord and Savior when he taught in this world by the mercy of God. It happened, then, that after his martyrdom he appeared to the brethren and warned them to restore, without delay, whatever portion of his ashes each one by devotion had carried away, so that they might be gathered together into the same place.

He also appeared to Æmilianus. He was accompanied by his deacons, and all wore the robe of glory. He rebuked the judge roundly, showing him the uselessness of what he had done, for these whom he saw in glory were those whom he thought to be buried in the earth.

O holy martyrs, proved by fire as precious gold covered with the breastplate of faith and the helmet of salvation, as the price of the victory over the devil whose head you have crushed, you have received a diadem and an imperishable crown!

O holy martyrs, you have merited a dwelling in heaven, standing on the right hand of Christ, blessing the Father Almighty and His Son our Lord Jesus Christ. God has received His martyrs in peace for their faithful confession. Glory and honor to Him forever. Amen.[2]

NOTES

1. "A station was the reunion of the faithful at some appointed spot for public prayer, recitation or psalms, etc. These stations probably originated before even the second century, and usually took the form of vigils. The liturgy here recited is the origin of the evening and night recitation of Vespers, Matins and Lauds – the most primitive part of the Roman office. These vigils were usually terminated by a stational Mass. The stations in Rome for many of the Masses are still indicated in the Roman Missal, and are observed on certain occasions."—This definition was taken from *Rome of the Pilgrims and Martyrs* by Ethel Ross Barker.
2. This English translation of *The Passion of Fructuosus* was originally published in *Rome of the Pilgrims and Martyrs* by Ethel Ross Barker.

CHAPTER 14

The Acts of Saints Chionia, Agape and Irene who Hid the Scriptures

Sometime in AD 260, the emperor Valerian suffered a major defeat at the hands of the Persian King Sapor I at the Battle of Edessa. During negotiations following the battle, Sapor broke the truce and took the emperor prisoner. According to the Christian scholar Lactantius, writing about fifty years later, Valerian, "having been made prisoner by the Persians, lost not only that power which he had exercised without moderation, but also the liberty of which be had deprived others. And he wasted the remainder of his days in the vilest condition of slavery."[1] It is said that Sapor used Valerian as a footstool when mounting his horse. After the disgraced emperor perished in captivity, Sapor caused his body to be flayed, dyed the skin bright red, and hung it in one of the temples in Ctesiphon, the Persian capital city, as a permanent memorial of his victory over the Romans.

With the capture of Valerian, his son and successor Gallienus ended the persecution initiated by his father. With the cessation of the persecution, Christians would again be left largely in peace for the next thirty years while the empire dealt with a crisis of unsurpassed magnitude. At this time, the Roman Empire came very close to flying apart at the seams. It was saved by the herculean efforts of several energetic but short-lived emperors, culminating in the advent of Diocletian in AD 284.

I AM A CHRISTIAN

Diocletian was a man of humble parentage who was born in the province of Dalmatia—modern day Croatia. He rose through the ranks of the Roman military and was named commander of the household guard of the emperor Carus. When Carus and his son Numerian perished after a victorious campaign in Persia, Diocletian found himself proclaimed emperor by the eastern armies. He successfully put down all challengers and was able to establish his rule over a unified Roman Empire.

Diocletian was known as a reformer who attempted to put the imperial government on a firmer footing. In many respects, he was successful in this effort. He established a system of dioceses within the empire, to replace the old provincial system. Recognizing that the empire was too vast to be ruled by one man alone, he appointed a trusted colleague, Maximian, as co-Augustus to rule in the West while he ruled the East. He further appointed two junior emperors or Cæsars, Galerius and Constantius Chlorus, to assist the two Augusti.

When it came to Christianity, however, Diocletian's idea of reform was to attempt to wipe out the Faith completely. At the instigation of his Cæsar Galerius, Diocletian imposed new punitive laws upon the Christians and pursued them with a vigor far beyond even Decius or Valerian. These laws included the loss of rank and status for those who professed Christ, the demolition of Christian churches, the surrender and destruction of the Christian Scriptures and holy books, and later, the imprisonment of all deacons, priests and bishops, and a mandate for all people to offer public sacrifice to the pagan gods. Lactantius, who lived through it, described the beginning of the persecution as follows:

> When that day dawned, in the eighth consulship of Diocletian and seventh of Maximian, suddenly, while it was yet hardly light, the prefect, together with chief commanders, tribunes, and officers of the treasury, came to the church in Nicomedia and the gates having been forced open, they searched everywhere for an image of the Divinity. The books of the Holy Scriptures were found, and they were committed to the flames. The utensils and furniture of the church were abandoned to pillage. All was rapine, confusion, tumult. That church, situated on rising ground, was within view of the palace, and Diocletian and Galerius stood, as

if on a watchtower, disputing long whether it ought to be set on fire. The sentiment of Diocletian prevailed, who dreaded lest so great a fire being once kindled, some part of the city might be burnt, for there were many and large buildings that surrounded the church. Then the Prætorian Guards came in battle array, with axes and other iron instruments, and having been let loose everywhere, they in a few hours levelled that very lofty edifice with the ground.²

From there, the persecution only gained in ferocity. Galerius hailed from the city of Thessalonica in Macedonia, so it is fitting that our first account of the Great Persecution comes from there. This transcript records the trial of three sisters—Agape, Chionia and Irene—and begins with the Roman authorities making two accusations against them, along with four other Christians. The charges were that they refused to eat meat that had been sacrificed to idols, and that they had hidden Christian books. This passage was taken from Butler's Lives of the Fathers, Martyrs, and Other Principal Saints, *"from their original acts, abridged out of the presidial court registers of Thessalonica."*

In the year 303, the emperor Diocletian published an edict forbidding, under pain of death, any persons to keep the holy scriptures. These saints concealed many volumes of these sacred books, but were not discovered or apprehended till the year following, when, as their acts relate, Dulcetius, the governor, being seated in his tribunal, Artemesius, the secretary, said: "If you please, I will read an information, given in by the Stationary, concerning several persons here present."

Dulcetius: "Let the information be read."

The solicitor read as follows: "The Pensioner Cassander to Dulcetius, president of Macedonia, greeting. I send to your highness six Christian women, with a man, who have refused to eat meats sacrificed to the gods. They are called Agape, Chionia, Irene, Casia, Philippa, Eutychia, and the man's name is Agatho.

Therefore I have caused them to be brought before you."

The president, turning to the women, said: "Wretches, what madness is this of yours, that you will not obey the pious commands of the emperors and Cæsars?" He then said to Agatho: "Why will you not eat of the meats offered to the gods, like other subjects of the empire?"

He answered: "Because I am a Christian."

Dulcetius: "Do you still persist in that resolution?"

Agatho: "Certainly."

Dulcetius next addressed himself to Agape, saying: "What are your sentiments?"

Agape answered: "I believe in the living God, and will not by an evil action lose all the merit of my past life."

Then the president said: "What say you, Chionia?"

She answered: "I believe in the living God, and for that reason did not obey your orders."

The president, turning to Irene, said: "Why did not you obey the most pious command of our emperors and Cæsars?"

Irene: "For fear of offending God."

President: "But what say you, Casia?"

Casia: "I desire to save my soul."

President: "Will not you partake of the sacred offerings?"

Casia: "By no means."

President: "But you, Philippa, what do you say?"

She answered: "I say the same thing."

President: "What is that?"

Philippa: "That I had rather die than eat of your sacrifices."

President: "And you, Eutychia, what do you say?"

Eutychia: "I say the same thing, that I had rather die than do what you command."

President: "Are you married?"

Eutychia: "My husband has been dead almost these seven months."

President: "By whom are you with child?"

Eutychia: "By him whom God gave me for my husband."

President: "I advise you, Eutychia, to leave this folly and

resume a reasonable way of thinking. What do you say? Will you obey the imperial edict?"

Eutychia: "No, for I am a Christian and serve the Almighty God."

President: "Eutychia being big with child, let her be kept in prison."

Afterwards Dulcetius added: "Agape, what is your resolution? Will you do as we do, who are obedient and dutiful to the emperors?"

Agape: "It is not proper to obey Satan. My soul is not to be overcome by these discourses."

President: "And you, Chionia, what is your final answer?"

Chionia: "Nothing can change me."

President: "Have you not some books, papers, or other writings, relating to the religion of the impious Christians?"

Chionia said: "We have none: the emperors now reigning have taken them all from us."

President: "Who drew you into this persuasion?"

She said, "Almighty God."

President: "Who induced you to embrace this folly?"

Chionia repeated again, "Almighty God, and his only Son our Lord Jesus Christ."

Dulcetius: "You are all bound to obey our most puissant emperors and Cæsars. But because you have so long obstinately despised their just commands, and so many edicts, admonitions, and threats, and have had the boldness and rashness to despise our orders, retaining the impious name of Christians. And since to this very time you have not obeyed the stationaries and officers who solicited you to renounce Jesus Christ in writing, you shall receive the punishment you deserve."

Then he read their sentence, which was worded as follows: "I condemn Agape and Chionia to be burnt alive, for having out of malice and obstinacy acted in contradiction to the divine edicts of our lords the emperors and Cæsars, and who at present profess the rash and false religion of Christians, which all pious persons abhor." He added: "As for the other four, let them be confined in close prison during my pleasure."

After these two had been consumed in the fire, Irene was a third time brought before the president.

Dulcetius: "Your madness to plain, since you have kept to this day so many books, parchments, codicils, and papers of the scriptures of the impious Christians. You were forced to acknowledge them when they were produced before you, though you had before denied you had any. You will not take warning from the punishment of your sisters, neither have you the fear of death before your eyes: your punishment therefore is unavoidable. In the meantime I do not refuse even now to make some condescension in your behalf. Notwithstanding your crime, you may find pardon and be freed from punishment, if you will yet worship the gods. What say you then? Will you obey the orders of the emperors? Are you ready to sacrifice to the gods, and eat of the victims?"

Irene: "By no means: for those that renounce Jesus Christ, the Son of God, are threatened with eternal fire."

Dulcetius: "Who persuaded you to conceal those books and papers so long?"

Irene: "Almighty God, who has commanded us to love him even unto death, on which account we dare not betray him but rather choose to be burnt alive or suffer any thing whatsoever than discover such writings."

President: "Who knew that those writings were in the house?"

Irene: "Nobody, but the Almighty, from whom nothing is hid: for we concealed them even from our own domestics, lest they should accuse us."

President: "Where did you hide yourselves last year, when the pious edict of our emperors was first published?"

Irene: "Where it pleased God, in the mountains."

President: "With whom did you live?"

Irene: "We were in the open air, sometimes on one mountain, sometimes on another."

President: "Who supplied you with bread?"

Irene: "God, who gives food to all flesh."

President: "Was your father privy to it?"

Irene: "No, he had not the least knowledge of it."

President: "Which of your neighbors knew it?"

Irene: "Inquire in the neighborhood, and make your search."

President: "After you returned from the mountains, as you say, did you read those books to anybody?"

Irene: "They were hid at our own house, and we durst not produce them. And we were in great trouble, because we could not read them night and day, as we had been accustomed to do."

Dulcetius: "Your sisters have already suffered the punishments to which they were condemned. As for you, Irene, though you were condemned to death before your flight for having hid these writings, I will not have you die so suddenly, but I order that you be exposed naked in a brothel, and be allowed one loaf a day, to be sent you from the palace, and that the guards do not suffer you to stir out of it one moment, under pain of death to them."

The infamous sentence was rigorously executed. But God protecting her, no man durst approach her, nor say or do any indecency to her. The president caused her to be brought again before him

President: "Do you still persist in your rashness?"

Irene: "Not in rashness, but in piety towards God."

Dulcetius: "You shall suffer the just punishment of your insolence and obstinacy."

And having called for paper, he wrote this sentence: "Since Irene will not obey the emperor's orders and sacrifice to the gods, but, on the contrary, persists still in the religion of the Christians, I order her to be immediately burnt alive, as her sisters have been."

Dulcetius had no sooner pronounced this sentence but the soldiers seized Irene and brought her to a rising ground where her sisters had suffered martyrdom, and having lighted a large pile, ordered her to mount thereon. Irene, singing psalms and celebrating the glory of God, threw herself on the pile and was there consumed in the ninth consulship of Diocletian, and the eighth of Maximian.[3]

The Roman Martyrology says that the martyrdom of Saints Agape and Chionia took place on April 3, with Saint Irene following on the 5th of April. The fates of Casia, Eutychia, Philippa and Agatho are unknown.

NOTES

1. This quote of Lactantius is taken from his treatise entitled, *Of the Manner in Which the Persecutors Died*, Chapter 5, translated into English by William Fletcher and originally published in *The Ante-Nicene Christian Library, Volume 12: The Works of Lactantius, Volume 2*.
2. This passage from Lactantius is also taken from *Of the Manner in Which the Persecutors Died*, Chapter 12.
3. The Acts of Chionia, Agape and Irene as presented here are taken from *Butler's Lives of the Primitive Fathers, Martyrs and Other Principal Saints, Volume IV*.

Chapter 15

"Traditores" and the Burning of Christian Books

As we have seen in the previous chapter, possessing or attempting to hide Christian holy books was considered a crime worthy of death. Diocletian and Galerius well knew that the Christian religion could not be completely stamped out unless its writings and records were destroyed. So for a period of about eight years in the early 4th century AD, it was mandated by edict that all Christian books be burned, and Roman authorities went door-to-door in certain cities searching for them.

Here is the mention of this edict from the Ecclesiastical History of Eusebius, written about 20–30 years after the event:

"It was the nineteenth year of Diocletian's reign [AD 303] and the month Dystrus, called March by the Romans, and the festival of the Savior's Passion was approaching, when an imperial decree was published everywhere, ordering the churches to be razed to the ground and the Scriptures destroyed by fire..."[1]

Early Christian churches often housed libraries of valuable scriptural, catechetical, and historical works. But because churches were easy targets for persecutors, copies of the Scriptures and other books were dispersed in the homes of the minor orders: subdeacons, lectors and even gravediggers. Even so, the pagan Roman authorities were very thorough, which is one of the reasons why so very few Christian historical documents and

I AM A CHRISTIAN

accounts dating prior to the 4th century, such as the ones presented in this book, have survived intact. Knowing that the Christians preserved trial transcripts of their martyrdoms, pagan Roman officials actively purged such accounts from their voluminous legal archives.

We know that the burning of Christian books by imperial mandate did happen thanks to investigatory reports and legal transcripts that have survived from the reign of Diocletian. These include the following Roman legal report taken in the city of Cirta in the African province of Numidia. This report was read out as part of a trial during the subsequent reign of Constantine in AD *320 and is drawn from the municipal acts of Cirta recorded by the curator Munatius Felix, a pagan.*

This transcript is interesting for at least three reasons. First, it corroborates that the persecution initiated by Diocletian and Galerius in the east, took place in Africa as well, which was a province under the control of the co-Augustus of the west, Maximian. Second, it reveals the level of thoroughness and stark detail that went into Roman legal reporting. Third, it demonstrates quite clearly that not all Christians died heroic deaths during the persecution. Indeed, many became "traditores" who willingly handed over the Sacred Scriptures to save their own lives.

Following is the full transcript dated May 19, AD *304.*

In the consulate of Diocletian the Eighth, and Maximian the Seventh, on the nineteenth of May, from the Acts of Munatius Felix the perpetual flamen, the guardian of the colony at Cirta.

When they came to the house in which the Christians were accustomed to assemble, Felix the flamen and guardian of the state said to Paul the Bishop: "Bring out the Scriptures of the Law and anything else that you may have here, as has been commanded, that you may obey the order."

Paul the Bishop said: "The lectors have the Scriptures. But we surrender what we have here."

Felix the perpetual flamen and guardian of the state said to Paul the Bishop: "Show us the lectors or send to them."

Paul the Bishop said: "You all know them."

Felix the perpetual flamen and guardian of the state said: "We do not know them."

Paul the Bishop said: "The public officers know them—that is Edusius and Junius, the notaries."

Felix the perpetual flamen and guardian of the state said: "Let the matter of the lectors stand over. They will be pointed out by the public officers. Do you surrender what you have."

In the presence of Paul the Bishop (who remained seated); of Montanus and Victor of Deusatelium, and Memorius, priests; Mars and Helius, the deacons; Marcuclius, Catullinus, Silvanus and Carosus, the subdeacons standing by with Januarius, Meraclus, Fructuosus, Migginis, Saturninus, Victor and the rest of the grave-diggers, Victor of Aufidus made this brief inventory against them:

Two golden chalices, also six silver chalices, six silver pots, a silver chafing vessel, seven silver lamps, two torches, seven short brass candlesticks with their lamps, also eleven brass candlesticks with their chains, eighty-two women's garments, thirty-eight veils, sixteen men's garments, thirteen pair of men's shoes, forty-seven pair of women's shoes, eighteen patens for the country.

Felix the perpetual flamen and guardian of the state said to Marcuclius, Silvanus and Carosus the grave-diggers: "Bring forth whatever you have."

Silvanus and Carosus said: "All that was here we have thrown out."

Felix the perpetual flamen and guardian of the state said to Marcuclius, Silvanus and Carosus: "Your answer is set down in the Acts."

After the cupboards in the bookcases had been found to be empty, Silvanus brought forth a silver casket, and a silver candlestick, for he said that he had found them behind a jug.

Victor of Aufidus said to Silvanus: "Had you not found these things, you were a dead man."

Felix the perpetual flamen and guardian of the state said to Silvanus: "Search more carefully, lest anything else should have been left behind."

Silvanus said: "Nothing has been left behind. This is all—what we have thrown out."

And when the dining-room was opened, there were found in it four casks and six jugs.

Felix the perpetual flamen and life-guardian of the state said: "Bring forth whatever Scriptures you have, that we may obey the precepts and commands of the emperors."

Catullinus brought forth one very large codex.

Felix the perpetual flamen and guardian of the state said to Marcuclius and Silvanus: "Why have you given us only one codex? Bring forth the Scriptures which you have."

Catullinus and Marcuclius said: "We have no more for we are sub-deacons, but the lectors have the codices."

Felix the perpetual flamen and guardian of the state said to Marcuclius and Catullinus: "Show us the lectors."

Marcuclius and Catullinus said: "We do not know where they live."

Felix the perpetual flamen and guardian of the state said to Catullinus and Marcuclius: "If you do not know where they are living, tell us their names."

Catullinus and Marcuclius said: "We are not traitors, behold we are here. Order us to be killed."

Felix the perpetual flamen and guardian of the state said: "Let them be taken into custody."

And when they came to the house of Eugenius, Felix the perpetual flamen and guardian of the state said to Eugenius: "Bring forth the Scriptures which you have, that you may obey the decree."

And he brought forth four codices.

Felix the perpetual flamen and guardian of the state said to Silvanus and Carosus: "Show us the other lectors."

Silvanus and Carosus said: "The Bishop has already told you that the notaries Edusius and Junius know them all. Let them point out their houses to you."

Edusius and Junius said: "We will point them out to you, my lord."

And when they came to the house of Felix, the worker in marbles, he brought forth five codices. And when they came to the house of Victorinus, he brought forth eight codices. And when they came to the house of Projectus, he brought forth five large and two small codices.

And when they came to the house of Victor the Grammarian, Felix the perpetual flamen and guardian of the state said to him: "Bring forth whatever Scriptures you have, that you may obey the decree."

Victor the Grammarian brought forth two codices, and four quinions. Felix the perpetual flamen and guardian of the state said to Victor: "Bring forth the Scriptures. You have more."

Victor the Grammarian said: "If I had more, I would have given them."

And when they came to the house of Euticius of Cæsarea, Felix the perpetual flamen and guardian of the state said to Euticius: "Bring forth the Scriptures which you have, that you may obey the decree."

Euticius said: "I have none."

Felix the perpetual flamen and guardian of the state said to Euticius: "Your statement is set down in the Acts."

And when they came to the house of Coddeo, his wife brought forth six codices.

Felix the perpetual flamen and guardian of the state then said: "Look and see whether you have not got more. Bring them forth."

The woman said: "I have no more."

Felix the perpetual flamen and guardian of the state said to Bos the public official: "Go in and search whether she has not any more."

The public official said: "I have searched and have not found anything else."

Felix the perpetual flamen and guardian of the state said to Victorinus, Silvanus and Carosus: "If anything has been kept back, the danger is yours."[2]

I AM A CHRISTIAN

NOTES

1. This quote is reproduced from *The Ecclesiastical History* of Eusebius Book VIII, Chapter 2 and is taken from *A Select Library of Nicene and Post-Nicene Fathers of the Christian Church, Volume I: Eusebius*, translated by Arthur C. McGiffert.
2. This transcript is taken from *Against the Donatists* by Saint Optatus as translated in *The Work of Saint Optatus, Bishop of Milevis, Against the Donatists*. More background information on the complex history of this fascinating transcript and how it came down to us may be found there.

Chapter 16

The Martyrs of Abitina

Given that Christianity had enjoyed relative peace and freedom for about four decades prior to the outbreak of the Great Persecution, it is perhaps not surprising that many Christians were caught off guard and surrendered willingly to the initial round of imperial demands, giving up books and buildings rather than losing their lives. But as the persecution ramped up, more dramatic sacrifices would be demanded.

The following is another martyrdom account from Roman north Africa, specifically the town of Abitina. In this account, we meet the Roman proconsul Anulinus who will reappear in the martyrdom of Crispina in the next chapter. Anulinus questions the 49 Christians of Abitina on two counts: that they held the "Dominicum"—that is, the feast of the Lord's Day or Sunday Holy Mass—and that they were hiding Christian holy books. In this passage, we see some equivocation on the part of the martyrs, but also a steadfastness under torture that was not seen in the previous chapter when the Christians of Cirta gave over their holy books with little complaint. It is noteworthy, however, that the bishop of the town had left his flock to suffer without him.

This excerpt is taken from a translation and modern interpretation found in Arthur James Mason's book, The Historic Martyrs of the Primitive Church *(1917). This record was probably edited by a Donatist during antiquity—that is, a member of an heretical sect which believed that there could be no repentance for traditores.*

I AM A CHRISTIAN

When the trumpet of war was sounded the glorious martyrs in the city of Abitina set up the standard of the Lord in the house of Octavius Felix. There they were duly celebrating the "Dominicum" that is, the Lord's service, the Eucharist, when they were seized by the magistrates of the city and by the commandant of the district in person.

The leader of the party was unhappily not the bishop of Abitina, for that prelate had betrayed his trust at the beginning of the persecution and had forfeited the allegiance of his flock. The heavens, so it was said, had on that occasion fought for the Scriptures, for when the bishop gave them up to be burnt, a furious storm of rain and hail came down and put out the fire. The faithful were chiefly kept together by the earnestness of a layman called Dativus, who was a decurion, or member of the senate of Carthage, and by the priest Saturninus and his family.

The forty-nine were first examined in the forum of Abitina by the curator, and joyfully confessed their faith. But the curator was not competent to go further with them and despatched them to Carthage, to the proconsul. Rejoicing to feel the chains upon their wrists, which were to them the earnest of better things to come, they sang all the way to the capital. There, on the 12th of February 304, they were presented to Anulinus, and the clerks of the court reported that they were charged with having held an assembly and celebrated the Dominicum, contrary to the imperial edict.

Anulinus began with Dativus. Dativus had answered the usual questions about his position and the like and had confessed that he was a Christian and had taken part in the service, and was already stretched upon the hobby-horse to make him say who it was that had got up the gathering, when another of the party, called Thelica, stood out and cried, "We are Christians. It was we who came together."

Thelica succeeded in turning the severity of the law to himself. He was placed on the instrument, and the torture began. Out of the midst of his tortures Thelica kept crying, "Thanks be to God! For Thy name's sake, O Christ the Son of God, deliver Thy servants."

The purpose of Anulinus with him, as with Dativus, was to extract from him the name of the ringleader. At last, when the pain became intolerable, the man shouted, "It was the priest Saturninus," and then added, "and all of us." He would not admit that any one of the number, not even the priest, had been more zealous and brave than the rest.

But he had given a name, and when the proconsul asked which Saturninus was, Thelica pointed him out. Every utterance of the tortured man was entered in the official acts. "You are doing wrong, unhappy men," he cried. "You are fighting against God. O God most high, consent not to their sin. You are sinning, unhappy men. You are striving against God." Then, perhaps addressing the Christians, he cried, "Keep the commandments of the most high God." Then again, "You are doing wrong, unhappy men, you are tearing in pieces the innocent. We are not murderers. We have done no crime. O God, have mercy. I thank Thee, O Lord. Grant me to bear suffering for Thy name. Deliver Thy servants out of the captivity of this world. I thank Thee. I cannot thank Thee enough."

When his sides were streaming with blood, he heard the voice of Anulinus saying to him, "You shall begin to feel what you have to undergo."

"To glory!" shouted the martyr. "I thank the God of kingdoms. The eternal kingdom appeareth! The incorruptible kingdom! O Lord Jesus Christ, we are Christians. We serve Thee. Thou art our hope. Thou art the Christian's hope. O God most holy, O God most high, O God almighty. We give Thee thanks for Thy name, O Lord God Almighty."

Thelica's bodily strength was exhausted. The proconsul said to him, "You would have done better to keep the commandments of the emperors and Cæsars."

He replied with unabated spirit, "I care for nothing but the law of God which I have learned. That is what I keep. For that I will die. In that I shall be perfected, and there is none beside it."

At last Anulinus gave the word to stop, and Thelica was taken back to prison.

Dativus all this while was suspended on his hobby-horse. Attention returned to him after the removal of Thelica. Again and again he repeated that he was a Christian, and had joined in the gathering. Then the brother of one of the female prisoners stepped forth with a grave accusation. He was a barrister and, though he afterwards adopted his sister's religion, he was at that time a heathen. Dativus, he said, though not a friend of the family, had come to the house while the girl's father was away from Carthage and while he himself was engaged in his studies, and had prevailed upon his sister Victoria and two other girls to run away with him to Abitina.

But Victoria would not listen to her brother's insinuations. With a Christian's freedom of speech, she burst forth and told the proconsul that no one had persuaded her to go to Abitina, that she had not gone there with Dativus, she could prove it by witnesses in the town. "I did all this of my own free will and choice," she said, "and I was at the gathering and celebrated the Dominicum with the brethren, because I am a Christian."

Dativus, amidst his tortures, answered the charge with the dignity of a senator. His one cry was, "O Lord Christ, let me not be confounded."

The proconsul bade the executioners to stop examining him on that point. Another accuser who attempted to take away his character was soon silenced. But after a while they began to ply Dativus again with the question, who had brought about the gathering for divine service.

He answered that there was more than one person. When the torture began again, he repeated his former prayer, that he might not be confounded, and then he said, "What have I done? Saturninus is our priest."

It was the second time that the priest had been mentioned, and the proconsul now turned to Saturninus and said, "You acted against the command of the emperors and Cæsars in bringing all these people together."

The priest replied, "We had no hesitation about celebrating the Dominicum."

"Why so?" asked Anulinus.

"Because the Dominicum cannot possibly be dropped," was the reply.

Directly it was uttered, Saturninus was hoisted to the horse which Thelica had left, opposite to that of Dativus. The torturers were still at work upon Dativus, but he seemed to be rather a spectator of his own tortures than a sufferer. At intervals he ejaculated, "Help me, O Christ, I beseech Thee. Have pity. Save my soul. Keep my spirit, that I may not be confounded. I beseech Thee, O Christ, grant me the power to endure."

The proconsul observed to him, "Belonging to this famous city, you ought rather to have drawn other people to a good mind instead of transgressing the commandment of the emperors and Cæsars."

But Dativus only exclaimed more loudly than before, "I am a Christian."

At length Anulinus cried "Hold," and Dativus was taken to the prison.

The horse upon which Saturninus was slung was still wet with the blood of Thelica. The proconsul asked him whether it was he who had gathered his fellow Christians together. "Yes," he said at first, and then modestly disclaimed the special honor, by adding, "I was present at the service."

A reader named Emeritus sprang forward and took up the challenge. "I am responsible," he cried. "The services have been held at my house."

But Anulinus refused to follow up the confession at once. He went on with the priest. "Why did you transgress the commandment, Saturninus?" he said.

Saturninus replied as before, "The Dominicum cannot be dropped. So the law orders."

Anulinus expostulated, "Still, you ought not to have disregarded the prohibition. You ought to observe it and not engage in things that are contrary to the emperors' command." The words were gentle enough, but they were the prelude to a fearful mangling of the elderly man's body.

Saturninus cried out, "I beseech Thee, O Christ, hear me. I thank Thee, O God," then, whether in prayer to God or in defiance to man, "Cause me to be beheaded," and again, "I beseech Thee, O Christ, have mercy. O Son of God, succor me."

Once more the proconsul asked him, "Why did you transgress the commandment?"

The priest's only answer was, "So the law orders. So the law teaches."

"Hold," said Anulinus, and sent him to prison, under the sentence which he had desired.

Anulinus was now able to attend to Emeritus. When he was fastened up, Anulinus said to him, "Were the meetings held in your house, in contravention of the emperors' commands?"

"Yes," he answered, "we have had the Dominicum in my house."

"Why did you let them come in?" asked the proconsul.

"Because they are my brothers," was the reply, "and I could not forbid them."

"But you ought to have forbidden them," Anulinus said.

"It was impossible," answered Emeritus, "for we cannot do without the Dominicum."

Then the torture began. A fresh executioner took the place of the former who was tired, and dealt vigorous strokes. Emeritus cried, "I beseech Thee, O Christ, help me. You are transgressing the commandment of God, you unhappy people."

"You ought not to have received them," persisted Anulinus.

"I could not help receiving my brothers," again replied the martyr.

"The order of the emperors and Cæsars comes first," Anulinus said.

"God," replied Emeritus, "is greater than the emperors. I beseech Thee, O Christ: I offer Thee praise, O Christ. O Lord, grant me endurance."

The proconsul suddenly asked him, "Have you any Scriptures in your house?"

"I have some," Emeritus replied, "but I have them in my heart."

"Have you any in your house or not?" said Anulinus.

"I have them in my heart," the reader replied. "Christ, I beseech Thee. Praise to Thee. Deliver me, O Christ. I suffer in Thy name. It is a short suffering, a willing suffering, O Christ. Lord, let me not be confounded."

"Hold," said Anulinus to the executioner. Then making a note of the confession of Emeritus in his note-book, along with the rest, he said, "You shall all pay the penalty you have deserved, according to your own admission."

The proconsul was heartily tired of his business, though he had not half finished it. The reader Felix, son of the priest Saturninus, was next put forward. Anulinus, addressing all the prisoners together said, "I trust that you will take the line of obedience to the commandment, that you may live."

A shout went up from the whole band, "We are Christians. We cannot but keep the holy law of the Lord, even to the shedding of our blood."

To the question whether he had attended the service or whether he had any Scriptures, Felix only answered that he was a Christian.

"I did not ask whether you are a Christian," said Anulinus, "but whether you took part in the gathering and whether you have any Scriptures."

"O foolish question," cries the ancient editor of the Acts. "As if a man could be a Christian without the Dominicum! As there can be no Dominicum without Christians, so there can be no Christian without the Dominicum."

The reply of Felix embraced both parts of the proconsul's question. "We had a glorious gathering. We have always come together for the Dominicum, to read the Scriptures of the Lord." The brave reader was so severely thrashed with sticks that he died of it, and so did another of the number who bore the same common name.

Another reader, Ampelius, answered in the words of Emeritus:

"I took part in the service with the brethren and celebrated the Dominicum. And I have the Scriptures of the Lord with me, but written in my heart. Christ, I offer Thee praise. Hear me, O Christ."

With nothing worse than a few blows about the neck, he went back to prison, "as if to the tabernacle of the Lord."

Rogatian confessed his faith and was sent to prison unhurt, Quintus and Maximian, after being belabored with sticks.

A third and more youthful Felix was beaten in like manner, crying loudly that the Dominicum is the hope and salvation of Christians. To the proconsul's question he answered, "Yes, I celebrated the Dominicum devoutly. I took part in the service with the brethren, for I am a Christian."

"And were you also present, Saturninus? " said the proconsul to the next man, who was a son of the priest and, like his brother Felix, a reader.

"I am a Christian," was his answer.

"I do not ask you that," said Anulinus, "but whether you did the Dominicum"

"I did," said Saturninus, "because Christ is our Savior."

Thereupon the young man was fastened upon the same hobby-horse from which his father had been taken down. When he was stretched ready for the torture, Anulinus said to him, "What do you propose, Saturninus? You see where you are? Have you any Scriptures?"

He answered, "I am a Christian."

"I ask you," said Anulinus, "whether you were at the meeting, and whether you have the Scriptures."

"I am a Christian," he replied. "There is no name besides Christ's that we ought to keep holy."

"Since you persist in your obstinacy," said the proconsul, "you must be tortured. Tell me whether you have any Scriptures."

Then turning to the officers, he said, "Torture him."

The claw, from which his father's blood had not been wiped, tore open the young man's sides, and at last he cried out, like others before him, that he had the Scriptures of the Lord, but in a place from which no violence could tear them, in his heart. "I beseech Thee, O Christ, grant me power to endure," he prayed, "my hope is in Thee."

"Why did you transgress the commandment?" asked Anulinus.

"Because I am a Christian," the young man answered. He was soon sent to rejoin his father in prison.

It was growing late in the day, and Anulinus was anxious to get on. Addressing the large band of Christians who were still to be dealt with, he said, "You have seen what those who persisted have borne, and what those who still persist will have to bear. Therefore let any one of you who wishes to obtain pardon, and to be saved, speak out."

"We are Christians," was the unanimous answer. And they were all sent back to prison under sentence of death. To two of them, however, was granted the honor of being separately questioned. One was the maiden Victoria, who had consecrated her virginity to Christ. The proconsul asked what her intentions were.

She answered firmly, "I am a Christian."

Her brother Fortunatian, who acted as her advocate, affirmed that she had been driven out of her mind with subtle arguments, but Victoria answered, "This is my mind. I have never changed it."

The proconsul was anxious to spare her. "Will you go with your brother Fortunatian?" he inquired.

"No," the maiden answered. "I am a Christian, and my brethren are those who keep the commandments of God."

Anulinus endeavored to persuade her. "Think what is for your good," he said, "you see your brother is desirous to provide for your safety."

"I have told you my mind," Victoria said. "I have never changed it, and I was at the service and celebrated the Dominicum with the brethren, for I am a Christian."

The last of the nine and forty was a little boy called Hilarian. He was the youngest child of the brave priest Saturninus. He had seen his father and one brother tortured, another brother beaten almost to death, and a maiden sister whose name was Mary, sent to prison to await martyrdom. The humane Anulinus thought to relieve the boy of responsibility for his action. "Did you follow your father or your brothers?" he asked.

But the boy saw through the artifice, and would neither incriminate them nor lose his own glory. He answered, "I am a Christian. It was of my own free will and choice that I took part in the service with my father and with the brethren."

Anulinus attempted to frighten him with ugly threats of injury without martyrdom. "I shall cut off your hair," he said, "and your nose, and your ears, and then let you go."

Hilarian answered boldly, "Do whatever you please, for I am a Christian."

The proconsul contended no further, but ordered him to prison along with the rest, under condemnation of death.

The court rang with the boy's answer: "Thanks be to God."[1]

NOTE

1. This lengthy transcript is taken from *The Acts of the 49 Martyrs of Abitina* as translated and interpreted in *The Historic Martyrs of the Primitive Church* by Arthur James Mason.

Chapter 17

The Passion of Saint Crispina

Being a member of the nobility was no guarantee of safety from the wrath of the Great Persecution. On December 5 of the year AD 304, a wealthy Roman matron of the north African city of Thagara named Crispina was executed for the crime of being a Christian. A transcript of her trial has come down to us, and it is considered authentic, owing to the subsequent fame of this martyr who was worthy to be named several times by Saint Augustine in sermons delivered about a century after her death. Indeed, in his Exposition on Psalm 120, Augustine testifies of Saint Crispina:

"Is there anyone in Africa who does not know about these events, brothers and sisters? Scarcely, for she was extremely famous, of noble stock and very wealthy."[1]

Indeed, her fame extended beyond Africa to Italy. There, her likeness can be seen to this day as part of the well-known mosaic precession of female martyrs in the nave of the basilica of Sant'Apollinare Nuovo in Ravenna—a work was originally created in the mid-6th century.

This short account of Saint Crispina's trial is taken from Saint Alphonsus de Ligouri's work entitled, Victories of the Martyrs, originally written in 1776. Saint Alphonsus referred to the ancient Acts when compiling his tract on Crispina. Her antagonist is the proconsul

Anulinus—the same as featured in the account of the martyrs of Abitina in the preceding chapter. This Anulinus would go on to become prefect of Rome under the usurper Maxentius, and would continue to serve during the reign of Constantine, though no longer as a persecutor.

Saint Crispina was held in high veneration all through Africa, and is honored by Saint Augustine in various parts of his works, in which he speaks of her martyrdom. She was a noble lady, very rich, and the mother of several children. When she found herself in danger of losing her children, her possessions, and her life in the persecution which was then raging, instead of being intimidated, she was filled with a holy joy, not unworthy of the Christian education which she had received from her most tender years.

Being arrested in her native city of Thagara by order of the proconsul Anulinus and brought before his tribunal, he inquired of her whether she was aware of the imperial edicts which commanded that all persons should sacrifice to the gods of the empire. She replied: "I have never sacrificed, nor will I sacrifice to any other than to the one God, and to our Lord Jesus Christ his Son, who was born and suffered for us."

Anulinus then said: "Leave this thy superstition and adore the gods."

"Every day," said Crispina, "I adore my God, and besides him I know of no others."

"I perceive now," said the judge, "that thou art obstinate, and dost contemn our gods: thou must be made to experience the rigor of the laws."

"I shall suffer most willingly," replied the saint, "whatever may be exacted as the testimony of my faith."

"I will give thee to read," said the proconsul, "the edict of the emperor, which it behooveth thee to observe."

The saint replied: "I observe the commands of my Lord Jesus Christ."

Anulinus: "But thou shalt lose thy head, unless thou wilt observe the commands of the emperor, as they are observed throughout Africa."

Crispina: "No one shall oblige me to sacrifice to demons. I sacrifice to the Lord only, who made heaven and earth."

Here the proconsul began to exhort her to obey the edicts and to avoid the terrible consequences of the emperor's wrath.

The saint courageously replied: "I fear not the anger of men. All they can do is nothing. I fear only God who is in heaven, and I should be lost forever were I to offend him by sacrilege."

"Thou shalt not," said the proconsul, "be guilty of that crime by obeying the princes and adoring the gods of the Romans."

But Crispina, raising her voice, exclaimed: "Wouldst thou then have me guilty of sacrilege before God, in order not to appear sacrilegious to the eyes of men? It never shall be! God alone is great and omnipotent, the Creator of all things. Men are his creatures. What, therefore, can they do?"

Anulinus, seeing that the saint continued firm in the faith, after some other invectives and threats, ordered that her head should be shaved, as a token of degradation, adding, that if she continued obstinate he would condemn her to a most cruel death.

The saint answered: "I care not for the present life, and am only anxious for the life of my soul. I fear eternal torments only."

"Instantly obey," exclaimed the proconsul, "or your head shall at once be struck off!"

The saint meekly answered: "I shall return thanks to my God, for making me worthy of this blessed lot. God is with me, that I may not consent to thy suggestions."

Here Anulinus exclaimed: "Why do we any longer bear with this impious woman?" Then, having caused the process of her trial to be read over, he pronounced the final sentence, that Crispina should lose her head for obstinately refusing to sacrifice to the gods in obedience to the edicts.

Crispina, having heard the iniquitous sentence, calmly and

with holy joy said: "I return thanks to Jesus Christ, and I bless the Lord who has vouchsafed thus to deliver me from the hands of men."

She consummated her martyrdom on the 5th December, about the year 304.[2]

NOTES

1. For the context of this quote, see Boulding: *The Works of Saint Augustine: A Translation for the 21st Century.* Expositions of the Psalms, 99–120.
2. This rendering of the Acts of Saint Crispina is recorded in *Victories of the Martyrs* by Saint Alphonsus Ligouri and was translated into English by Eugene Grimm.

Chapter 18

Saint Agnes of Rome

From Africa, we return to the Eternal City itself—Rome—where the avaricious and merciless Maximian Herculius reigned as Augustus. It is thought that the Great Persecution raged with somewhat less ferocity here than in the east and Africa, not due to any goodwill on the part of Maximian, but because he was busy despoiling senators and the petty nobility of their wealth. Nonetheless, Lactantius tells us that Maximian, "*enforced the edicts throughout his dominions of Italy.*"[1]

Among the martyrs of Rome during this time, the name of Saint Agnes is one of the most famous. A young girl of perhaps 12 or 13 at the time of her martyrdom, Agnes would later be commemorated in the Roman Canon of the Mass. Though no authentic account of her trial is known to have survived antiquity, the passion of Saint Agnes is known from three near contemporary ancient sources.

The first is an epitaph which was affixed to her tomb in the catacombs by Pope Damasus in the late 4th century AD. The marble slab containing this epitaph may be seen to this day at the basilica of Saint Agnes in Rome. The second source is a homily given by Saint Ambrose of Milan, also in the late 4th century. The third is yet another poem from the faithful Prudentius in his collection known as the **Peristephanon**, *again from the same time period about 80 years after the death of Agnes. Prudentius's poem contains additional details, some of which are certainly exaggerated for poetic effect. But all three of these sources corroborate the principal facts of Saint Agnes's martyrdom and bear witness to her extraordinary passion and death.*

Saint Agnes, martyr: Epitaph by Pope Damasus

> Report says that when she had recently been snatched away from her parents, when the trumpet pealed forth its terrible clangor, the virgin Agnes suddenly left the breast of her nurse and willingly braved the threats and rage of the tyrant who wished to have her noble form burned in flames. Though of so little strength she checked her extreme fear, and covered her naked members with her abundant hair lest mortal eye might see the temple of the Lord. O thou dear one, worthy to be venerated by me! O sacred dignity of modesty! Be thou favorable, I beseech thee, O illustrious martyr, to the prayers of Damasus![2]

Homily *Concerning Virginity* by Ambrose of Milan

> My task begins favorably, that since today is the birthday of a virgin, I have to speak of virgins, and the treatise has its beginning from this discourse. It is the birthday of a martyr, let us offer the victim. It is the birthday of Saint Agnes, let men admire, let children take courage, let the married be astounded, let the unmarried take an example. But what can I say worthy of her whose very name was not devoid of bright praise? In devotion beyond her age, in virtue above nature, she seems to me to have borne not so much a human name as a token of martyrdom, whereby she showed what she was to be...
>
> ...She is said to have suffered martyrdom when twelve years old. The more hateful was the cruelty which spared not so tender an age, the greater in truth was the power of faith which found evidence even in that age. Was there room for a wound in that small body? And she who had no room for the blow of the steel had that wherewith to conquer the steel. But maidens of that age are unable to bear even the angry looks of parents and are wont to cry at the pricks of a needle as though they were wounds. She was fearless under the cruel hands of the executioners, she was unmoved by the heavy weight of the creaking chains, offering her whole body to the sword of the raging soldier as yet ignorant of

death but ready for it. Or if she were unwillingly hurried to the altars, she was ready to stretch forth her hands to Christ at the sacrificial fires, and at the sacrilegious altars themselves to make the sign of the Lord the Conqueror, or again to place her neck and both her hands in the iron bands, but no band could enclose such slender limbs.

A new kind of martyrdom! Not yet of fit age for punishment but already ripe for victory, difficult to contend with but easy to be crowned, she filled the office of teaching valor while having the disadvantage of youth. She would not as a bride so hasten to the couch, as being a virgin she joyfully went to the place of punishment with hurrying step, her head not adorned with plaited hair but with Christ. All wept, she alone was without a tear. All wondered that she was so readily prodigal of her life, which she had not yet enjoyed, and now gave up as though she had gone through it. Everyone was astounded that there was now one to bear witness to the Godhead, who as yet could not, because of her age, dispose of herself. And she brought it to pass that she should be believed concerning God, whose evidence concerning man would not be accepted. For that which is beyond nature is from the Author of nature.

What threats the executioner used to make her fear him, what allurements to persuade her, how many desired that she would come to them in marriage! But she answered: "It would be an injury to my Spouse to look on any one as likely to please me. He who chose me first for Himself shall receive me. Why are you delaying, executioner? Let this body perish which can be loved by eyes which I would not."

She stood, she prayed, she bent down her neck. You could see the executioner tremble as though he himself had been condemned, and his right hand shake, his face grow pale as he feared the peril of another, while the maiden feared not for her own. You have then in one victim a twofold martyrdom, of modesty and of religion. She both remained a virgin and she obtained martyrdom.[3]

Saint Agnes by Prudentius

Within the walls of Rome is laid
Agnes, brave martyr, holy maid;
Twice blest, a martyr's death to die
And to preserve her chastity.
'Tis said, as yet of tender age,
  But strong in love, that she defied
The edict and the prætor's rage,
  Still faithful to the Crucified.
By threats and blandishments assailed
In vain, she wavered not nor quailed;
Dauntless and resolute, whate'er
Man's malice can devise to bear.
Then spake the judge: "This stubborn maid
May hold life cheap, nor be afraid
To bear the lash, and yet may be
Chary of her virginity.
Unless the maiden will incline
Her head before Minerva's shrine,
Fling her among the vile to be
A toy for foulest ribaldry!"
She said, "I am not left alone:
Christ will not so forget his own.
Bloodstained the sword will be—but I,
Christ helping me, unstained shall die."

Unscathed she faced it all—for none
Was bold to fix his gaze upon
Her comeliness, but turned away
Awestricken, and as those who pray.

Then cried the prætor, "Headsman, come!
The culprit has deserved her doom."

Saint Agnes of Rome

But when she saw him standing near,
   The headsman with his naked blade,
Then with a spirit void of fear,
   "Be praise to God," the maiden said.
"Far better, grim and pitiless,
   Thus, thus to woo me with thy sword,
Than with a smile and soft caress
   To tempt me to forsake my Lord.
Thine ardor makes me not afraid;
   Nor would I interpose delay,
I bare my bosom to thy blade —
   Quick, sheathe it in my heart, I pray!
O! Father, ope Thy gates to me!
O! Christ, I come, Thy bride, to Thee!"
Then low she bowed her gentle head,
   That swiftly so the sword might fall;
And swiftly so her spirit fled
   Obedient to the heavenly call.

Free and exultant soars on high
Her spirit, flashing through the sky,
Starlike, a bright, angelic band
Fit escort on her either hand.
This world of ours she sees below,
Far as the downward glance can go
Through earth's dank vapors, in the swirl
And turmoil of its dizzy whirl,
Herself in brightness; thence she views,
What empty phantoms man pursues.
The pride, the pomp of earthly things,
The stately palaces of kings,
The din, the tumult of the mart,
The silken pageantries of art,
The thousand troubles that annoy,
Long hours of sadness, fleeting joy,
The maddening thirst for gold, whereby
For paltry gains men cheat and lie,

And, worse, the envy turning all,
Which sweetest else might be, to gall;
These, as the night before the day,
Fast from her gazing fade away.

O! happy Agnes, thus to rise
On wings of glory through the skies!

O! happy thus without a stain
Thy maiden brightness to retain!

For all things to the pure are pure,
And they are blessèd, who endure.[4]

NOTES

1. For the context of this quote, see Chapter 15 of Lactantius's work, *Of the Manner in Which the Persecutors Died*, translated into English by William Fletcher and originally published in *The Ante-Nicene Christian Library, Volume 12: The Works of Lactantius, Volume 2*.
2. This epitaph of Damasus in English translation may be found in *Christian Archaeology* by Charles Wesley Bennett. Other epitaphs of Damasus are included in the Appendix of the current volume.
3. This passage is an excerpt from a homily of Saint Ambrose of Milan entitled *Concerning Virginity*, Book I, Chapter II as translated in *A Select Library of Nicene and Post-Nicene Fathers of the Christian Church, Volume X: Saint Ambrose*.
4. This poem from the *Peristephanon* of Prudentius was translated by I. Gregory Smith and may be found in Francis St. John Thackeray's *Translations from Prudentius*.

CHAPTER 19

Martyrdom Poems of Prudentius

As a climax to the Great Persecution of Diocletian, we offer three additional poems from the Peristephanon of Prudentius. Aurelius Prudentius Clemens was born in Spain in AD 348. We learn from his poems that he visited Rome during his life, but of the personal incidents of his career very little is known. Trained as a lawyer, he practiced his profession for some years, and filled important judicial posts, later receiving an appointment to a high position at the imperial court. A change came over him later in life and he resolved to devote the remainder of his days to the service of God and the composition of sacred poetry.

Unlike the works of Prudentius included in the previous chapters, the poems in this chapter represent the earliest or principal accounts of martyrs for whom no other near contemporary accounts survive. Of the three works presented here, two of them describe martyrdoms which took place in Prudentius's homeland, the Spanish provinces of the Roman Empire.

Eulalia was a young girl from Emerita, present-day Mérida in Western Spain. She was probably about the same age as Saint Agnes when she suffered. The account offered in Prudentius's poem is the oldest extant record of her passion.

The Martyrs of Calahorra, Saints Emeterius and Celedonius, were Roman soldiers killed for refusing to offer sacrifice to the pagan gods. Again, this poem is the only near-contemporary account of their acts.

Interesting to note, Prudentius himself mentions why no other official record of their martyrdom has survived, hearkening to the "oblivion of a silent age" whose testimonies were annihilated because "the infidel long since destroyed the page which...taught us how a martyr bleeds." This gives a hint of the level of success achieved by Diocletian's campaign to extirpate Christian literature.

Saint Quirinus, meanwhile, provides an exemplar of martyrdom from Roman Pannonia where he was bishop of the city of Sescia, now Sisak in modern-day Croatia. It is supposed that his death took place later than the others, in AD *309, after Diocletian had resigned his office and his protege Galerius reigned as Augustus in the East.*

It is worth noting at this point that none of the extant martyrdom accounts from the Great Persecution take place in the provinces of Britain or Gaul. This is because these provinces were the dominions of the Cæsar Constantius Chlorus who, though a worshipper of the pagan god Sol Invictus, had no appetite for executing Christians. The persecutory edicts enjoined upon him by Diocletian and Maximian were only partially enacted in his provinces and with little apparent enthusiasm.

Constantius Chlorus was the father of Constantine via his first wife, a woman who would be known to history as Saint Helena.

SAINT EULALIA BY PRUDENTIUS

> Born of a noble race,
> More by her death ennobled, Eulalie
>   Still by her dost on Merida sheds grace,
> Still dowers it with her filial piety.
>
>   A region in the West
> There lies, in men and in its city's pride
>   Rich, in its Virgin-Martyr still more blest,
> Than in all other braveries aside.
>
>   How brief her span of years!
> But thrice four winters had the maiden seen,
>   When welcoming the stake, she filled with fears
> Death's pursuivants by stern undaunted mien.

Proof early had she given
Of high emprise, to reach the Father's throne,
  No earthly bride, but dedicate to Heaven;
E'en childhood's toys and rattles were foregone.

  Roses were left disdained,
And necklace-amber: grave of aspect, staid,
  And wrapt in deepest musing she attained
Ripe wisdom of old age, this gentle maid.

  Hark how the crackling fires,
Driven against cheek and brow, with fiercer breath
  Feed on her locks and tower in wreathed spires!
She courts the flames, and drinks the longed-for death.

  'Tis said you then might see
Dart sudden from her lips a snow-white dove,
  The spirit pure of guileless Eulalie,
Winging its eager way to realms above.

  Ye boys and maidens, cull
Violet and crocus with its sanguine hues;
  That genial clime shall heap your baskets full,
Where Spring to burst the soil doth earlier use.

  Shed on her flowers and leaves!
Take these my dactyls—take my humble gift—
  A poor and withered wreath my music weaves
E'en these may grace the Feast, and hearts uplift.

  So we these relics prize,
This altar-slab in reverence we hold.
  Touched by my song, where at God's feet she lies,
She marks, and doth her own in love enfold.[1]

I AM A CHRISTIAN

Martyrs of Calahorra by Prudentius

In honor of the holy martyrs Emeterius and Celedonius

Inscribed in heaven two martyrs' names appear,
    Written by Christ in characters of gold;
The same were read in gory letters here,
    And Spain the wreath triumphantly doth hold.

God hath vouchsafed this place their bones should keep,
    And to their bodies sepulture accord,
Which the warm tide of blood imbib'ed deep,
    That from their twofold martyrdom outpoured.

The neighboring folk who now inhabit there,
    Where that most holy blood sank in the sands,
Visit the spot with vows and gifts and prayer,
    For Rumor spreadeth wide throughout all lands

That in this place the world's great patrons be,
    From whom true prayers an answer never lack;
No man in vain addresses them; for see
    With dried up tears he joyfully goes back,

Feeling that every just request be heard;
    Such aid to us those intercessors bring,
Of prayer forgetting not a whispered word,
    Straightway they bear it to the Eternal King.

And from the very source they can obtain
    Abundant gifts, bright waters that diffuse
The healing needed for each suppliant's pain:
    Christ to His martyrs nothing can refuse—

Martyrs whom neither bonds nor cruel death
    From the confessing of One God could fright,
At cost of blood; but thus to lose life's breath
    Is well repaid by a far longer light.

Such death is splendid—worthy of the good—
    To give unto the sword a network thin
Of woven veins, full surely else the food
    Of dull disease; and dying, victory win.

'Tis joy to feel the persecutor's knife,
    A noble gate the wound doth open wide
Unto the just, whose soul leaps forth to life,
    In that red fountain washed and purified.

As soldiers they full many a toil had known,
    But, tried in warfare, now they serve the shrine;
Instead of sash, Christ's *cingulum* they put on;
    The Cross, not Cæsar's flag, they choose for sign.

Nor the proud dragon-standard now uprear,
    But the bright Wood which did the dragon quell;
They now disdain to wield the bloody spear,
    Dig trench, or batter wall with engine fell.

It happened then from this world's haughty lord
    To Israel's second offspring orders came,
At altars where black idols were adored
    To sacrifice, and so deny the name.

Of Christ their King. Fury, begirt with steel,
    Threatened free Faith; but she, unscared, desired
The scourge and axe and double hooks to feel;
    The imprisoned neck hard chains in dungeon tired.

The torturer's hands now ply their cruel trade
    O'er all the forum wide; the voice of faith
Stifling in blood: sank virtue 'neath the blade,
    Or on the pile imbibed the flames of death.

To die by fire the just great sweetness found,
    And sweet to feel the sword's unpitying stroke.
Two brethren's hearts thus kindling, who were bound
    Throughout their life by friendship's dearest yoke,

They stand prepared to suffer any fate:
    To bow their neck the headsman's axe beneath,
After the echoing scourge or fiery grate,
    By leopards to be torn, or lion's teeth.

"Shall we, Christ's sons, the form of God who wear,
    Be this world's slaves, in Mammon's bonds confined
Oh, mingle not heaven's beams with darksome air!
    Suffice it that our early life, consigned

To Cæsar's service, paid the debt entire
    Of our first covenant; now 'tis time to pay
To God the things of God. Hence, ensigns dire!
    And you, ye tribunes, take yourselves away!

And the gold collars take away with you.
    Of wounds in battle once the recompense;
In white-clad cohorts to the soldiers true
    Of Christ, bright angel-hosts do call us hence.

He, yonder reigning on His lofty throne,
    Those foul and silly idols doth condemn,
Whom, fashioning to yourselves, for gods you own,
    And you, their foolish worshippers, with them."

And thus they spake, at once a thousand pains
    Those holy martyrs whelm on every side;
Their hands are manacled in galling chains,
    Their necks in weighty iron gorgets tied.

But oh, the oblivion of a silent age!
    Extinguishing the record of such deeds,
The infidel long since destroyed the page,
    Which else had taught us how a martyr bleeds,

Envying to learned times that they should tell
    That passion's history for all future years,
The order, time, and way how it befell—
    Sweet words to sound forever in men's ears.

Yet this alone is what we cannot say,
    Whether, in prison pent, their hair grew long,
Or of their torments reckon the array—
    One fact remains, in memory fresh and strong,

That certain gifts were wafted to the sky,
    Which their path thither plainly did portent.
Of one gold ring, faith's emblem, flew on high;
    And from the other did a scarf ascend,

Token of prayer. Breeze-borne, in depth of light
    Soon hides itself from view the gleaming gold,
And the white woof escapes the eager sight,
    Amid the stars men cannot it behold.

This all the people saw; the torturer saw,
    And in amaze he stayed his hand awhile,
And at the miracle turned pale with awe—
    Then smote he, not to lose his guerdon vile.

Believe ye now, ye Vascons,[2] I though possessed
    By error once, how pure the blood that fell
From those two victims, now with God at rest?
    See, how that holy blood can demons quell,

Who, like devouring wolves, men's hearts beset,
    Mix with the senses, choke the very soul;
Filled with his enemy, a man is set,
    He foams in rage, his fierce eyes he doth roll.

Relief is sought for him—not his the blame
    Of what he suffers; thou mayst hear him cry,
But see no torturing hand. How quails his frame,
    As it were lashed, and yet no scourge is nigh!

Stretched out he is with cords you cannot see.
    The martyr thus the demon vexeth much.
He tortures, burns him, chains him, so that he
    Is fain to drop the body from his clutch,

And quits the marrow in which he did lurk,
  Leaving his rescued prey all safe and well,
No trace, from head to foot, of his foul work,
  But owns himself to burn in fires of hell.

Why talk of bodies healed from long disease,
  Of swollen features unto form renewed?
Of some restored who ague-chill did freeze—
  Pale cheeks again with hues of health imbued?

This blessing on us did our Lord bestow,
  When to these martyrs sepulture He gave
In this our town, beside bright Ebro's flow—
  From many an ill can they their people save.

Sing now, ye mothers, for your children's sake,
  A hymn of praise: let the procession stand.
Matrons, thanksgiving for your husbands make—
  Be this a day of joy throughout the land.[3]

Saint Quirinus by Prudentius

Within the walls of Sisak,
  As in a sire's embrace,
God willed his faithful martyr
  Should witness to his grace.
So when the stern Galerius
  Oppressed th' Illyrian sea,
Quirinus there, with sword and prayer,
  Won truest victory.

Not by the steel relentless;
  Not by the fire's fierce breath;
Not by the paw and tooth of beast,
  Won he the meed of death.
No matter if by water;

No matter if by blood;
Death with equal glory
　　Appears in either flood.
So in the river's bosom,
　　Washed by the tender wave
That laid him down, he gained the crown
　　That marks the martyr's grave.

They bear him where the Savus
　　Beneath the bridge runs deep;
They tear him from his people—
　　The shepherd from his sheep.
About his neck they fasten,
　　That he may surely drown,
O, cruel fate, a millstone great,
　　To drag him swiftly down.

The whirlpool spreads its circles,
　　And bears him on its breast:
He and the mighty millstone
　　Lie there in quiet rest.
But now the martyr bishop,
　　Who waits the victor's palm
Feels even death denied him
　　In this most holy calm:
Death and the sure ascension,
　　That wellnigh seemed his own;
The opening skies to wistful eyes;
　　Th' Eternal Father's throne.

"O, Jesus, Lord, all-powerful,"
　　He cries, "not new to Thee
This triumph o'er the waters,
　　For Thou canst quell the sea:
Thine own apostle Peter,
　　Whom Thy right hand did keep,
Unyielding found, as solid ground,
　　The pathway of the deep.

I AM A CHRISTIAN

This stream Thy power proclaimeth,
   In bearing up a stone;
Grant me this boon, O Christ my God,
   To die for Thee alone!"
He praying thus is answered,
   And voice and vital flame,
Leaving the mortal body,
   Ascend to whence they came:
The stone again is heavy;
   The water's tender breast
Yields to his prayer and lays him there,
   In sweet and perfect rest.

NOTES

1. This poem of Prudentius was taken from the *Peristephanon* and may be found in Francis St. John Thackeray's *Translations from Prudentius*.
2. An ancient tribe in Spain which pre-dated the arrival of the Romans. It is supposed that they are the ancestors of the modern-day Basques.
3. This translation of Prudentius's *The Martyrs of Calahorra* (another work included in the *Peristephanon*) was found in *The Month: A Magazine and Review*, May-June, 1873 as part of an article entitled "A Hymn of Prudentius" by an anonymous translator.
4. Prudentius's poem on Saint Quirinus was taken from *Translations from Prudentius* and was translated in paraphrase by R. F. Towndrow.

CHAPTER 20

The Persian Martyrs

In AD 305, Diocletian suddenly abdicated the imperial throne in the East and forced Maximian to do likewise in the West. Galerius and Constantius were made senior emperors, and other men were chosen to be Cæsars. But the political solution Diocletian had envisioned to ensure the peaceful transition of power failed miserably. Within a short time, Constantius passed away and his son, Constantine, was made emperor by his father's soldiers in Ebaracum in Britain—present day York. With his advent and the simultaneous rise of his competitor in Rome, Maxentius, son of Maximian, the persecution of Christianity was tabled in the West while political matters took precedence. Then, in AD 312 as Constantine marched to grapple with Maxentius for mastery in the West, something momentous and utterly unexpected happened that would forever alter the course of history. Here is how Eusebius described the event which was related to him by Constantine himself and confirmed with an oath:

> "About mid-day, when the sun was beginning to decline, [Constantine] saw with his own eyes the trophy of a cross of light in the heavens, above the sun, and bearing the inscription, CONQUER BY THIS. At this sight he himself was struck with amazement, and his whole army also, which happened to be following him on some expedition, and witnessed the miracle."[1]

After witnessing this vision, Constantine caused Christian symbols to be affixed to his standards and won a stunning victory over Maxentius, *becoming in the process the sole ruler of the Western Empire.*

In the east, Galerius continued to press the persecution to its utmost until AD *311 when most suddenly, he was attacked by a dreadful and incurable disease. Lactantius describes the culmination of this horrifying illness as follows:*

> "The distemper attacked his intestines, and worms were generated in his body. The stench was so foul as to pervade not only the palace, but even the whole city—and no wonder, for by that time the passages from his bladder and bowels, having been devoured by the worms, became indiscriminate, and his body, with intolerable anguish, was dissolved into one mass of corruption."[2]

In terrible torment with his death fast approaching, Galerius issued an edict officially ending the Great Persecution. Constantine would follow up two years later with the famous Edict of Milan which not only confirmed toleration of Christianity throughout the Roman Empire, but aimed to right the many wrongs that had been done to Christians over the previous decade.

With the rise of Constantine, the systematic persecution of Christians which began under Diocletian came to an end. Never again would Roman Christians be subject to a systematic empire-wide attack, and the Christian religion, with Constantine as its standard-bearer, was now well on its way to becoming the official Faith of the Roman Empire.

However, at the same time Christianity was enjoying imperial favor in the Roman world, a great persecution erupted in neighboring Persia about the year AD *330. Constantine himself had written a letter to the Persian king, Sapor II, following an embassy, commending the Christian religion to his fellow ruler. However, some within the Persian court—and eventually Sapor himself—came to view the sudden rise of Christianity as a dire threat that needed to be extirpated from the realm. It is intriguing to compare the subsequent persecution experienced by the Persian Christians with that of the Roman Christians of a generation before.*

Presented below are several passages from the Ecclesiastical History of Hermias Sozomen, written about a century after the events they describe. A native of Roman Palestine, Sozomen was a third-generation Christian who had served as a lawyer in Constantinople, the eastern capital. His passages here show the impact of Constantine's conversion on religious politics of rival Persia. Whereas Christianity was once tolerated in Persia because Christians were considered fellow enemies of the Roman Empire, they were now viewed as agents of the Christian Roman state.

These passages also hint at how widely Christianity had spread within the domains of Sapor II as several Christians were found occupying high positions in Sapor's own court. Several poignant martyrdom accounts are offered, and Sozomen estimates the total numbers killed, saying that 16,000 had been recorded, but innumerable others had not been recorded.[1]

ACCOUNT OF THE PERSIAN PERSECUTION
FROM THE *ECCLESIASTICAL HISTORY* OF SOZOMEN

Book II, Chapter 9

When in course of time the Christians increased in number, assembled as churches, and appointed priests and deacons, the Magi, who had from time immemorial acted as priests of the Persian religion, became deeply incensed against them. The Jews who, through envy, are in some way naturally opposed to the Christian religion, were likewise offended. They therefore brought accusations before Sapor, the reigning sovereign, against Symeon who was then archbishop of Seleucia and Ctesiphon, royal cities of Persia, and charged him with being a friend of the Caesar of the Romans and with communicating the affairs of the Persians to him.

Sapor believed these accusations and at first imposed intolerably oppressive taxes upon the Christians, although he knew that the generality of them had voluntarily embraced poverty. He appointed cruel men to exact these taxes, hoping that by the want of necessaries and the atrocity of the tax-gatherers, they might be compelled to abjure their religion, for this was his aim.

Afterwards, however, he commanded that the priests and ministers of God should be slain with the sword. The churches were demolished, their vessels were deposited in the treasury, and Symeon was arrested as a traitor to the kingdom and the religion of the Persians. Thus the Magi, with the co-operation of the Jews, quickly destroyed the houses of prayer. Symeon, on his apprehension, was bound with chains and brought before the king. There he evinced the excellence and firmness of his character, for when Sapor commanded that he should be led away to the torture, he did not fear and would not prostrate himself.

The king, greatly exasperated, demanded why he did not prostrate himself as he had done formerly. Symeon replied that formerly he was not led away bound, in order that he might abjure the truth of God, and therefore did not then object to pay the customary respect to royalty. But that on the present occasion it would not be proper for him to do so, for he stood there in defense of godliness and of the one true faith. When he ceased speaking, the king commanded him to worship the sun, promising as an inducement to bestow gifts upon him and to raise him to honor, but on the other hand threatening, in case of noncompliance, to visit him and the whole body of Christians with destruction. When the king found that promises and menaces were alike unavailing, and that Symeon firmly refused to worship the sun or to betray his religion, he remanded him to prison, probably imagining that if kept for a time in bonds, he would change his mind.

When Symeon was being conducted to prison, Usthazanes, an aged eunuch, the foster-father of Sapor and superintendent of the palace who happened to be sitting at the gates of the palace, arose to do him reverence. Symeon reproachfully forbad him in a loud and haughty voice, averted his countenance, and passed by, for the eunuch had been formerly a Christian but had recently yielded to authority and worshipped the sun. This conduct so affected the eunuch, that he wept aloud, laid aside the white garment with which he was robed, and clothed himself as a mourner in black. He then seated himself in front of the palace, crying and groaning, and saying, "Woe is me! What must not await me? For I have denied God, and on this account Symeon, formerly my familiar friend, does not think me worthy of being spoken to, but turns away and hastens from me."

When Sapor heard of what had occurred, he called the eunuch to him and inquired into the cause of his grief and asked him whether any calamity had befallen his family. Usthazanes replied and said, "O king, nothing has occurred to my family but I would rather have suffered any other affliction whatsoever than that which has befallen me. Now I mourn because I am alive and ought to have been dead long ago. Yet I still see the sun which, not voluntarily but to please thee, I professed to worship. Therefore, on both accounts, it is just that I should die, for I have been a betrayer of Christ and a deceiver of thee." He then swore by the Maker of heaven and earth that he would never swerve from his convictions.

Sapor, astonished at the wonderful conversion of the eunuch, was still more enraged against the Christians as if they had effected it by enchantments. Still, he compassionated the old man and strove by alternate gentleness and severity to bring him over to his own sentiments. But finding that his efforts were useless and that Usthazanes persisted in declaring that he would never have the folly to worship the creature instead of the Creator, he became inflamed with passion and commanded that the eunuch's head should be struck off with a sword.

When the executioners came forward to perform their office, Usthazanes requested them to wait a little that he might communicate something to the king. He then called upon a certain faithful eunuch to convey the following address to Sapor: "From my youth until now I have been well affected, O king, to your house, and have ministered with care and diligence to your father and yourself. I need no witnesses to corroborate my statements, these facts are well established. For all the matters wherein at divers times I have gladly served you, grant me this reward—let it not be imagined by those who are ignorant of the circumstances that I have incurred this punishment by acts of unfaithfulness against the state or by the commission of any other crime, but let it be published and proclaimed abroad by a herald that Usthazanes loses his head for no crime that he has ever committed in the palace, but for being a Christian and for refusing to obey the king in denying his own God."

The eunuch delivered this message, and Sapor, according to the request of Usthazanes, commanded a herald to make the desired proclamation. The king imagined that others would be easily deterred from embracing Christianity by reflecting that he who sacrificed his aged foster-father and esteemed household servant would assuredly spare no other Christian. Usthazanes, however, believed that as by his timidity in consenting to worship the sun he had caused many Christians to fear, so now by the diligent proclamation of the cause of his sufferings, many might be edified by learning that he died for the sake of religion and so become imitators of his fortitude.

Book II, Chapter 10

In this manner the honorable life of Usthazanes was terminated, and when the intelligence was brought to Symeon in the prison, he offered thanksgiving to God on his account. The following day, which happened to be the sixth day of the week and likewise the day on which, as immediately preceding the festival of the resurrection, the annual memorial of the passion of the Savior is celebrated, the king issued orders for the decapitation of Symeon, for he had been again conducted to the palace from the prison, had reasoned most boldly with Sapor on points of doctrine, and had expressed a determination never to worship either the king or the sun.

On the same day a hundred other prisoners were ordered to be slain. Symeon beheld their execution, and last of all he was put to death. Amongst these victims were bishops, presbyters, and other clergy of different grades. As they were being led out to execution, the chief of the Magi approached them and asked them whether they would preserve their lives by conforming to the religion of the king and by worshipping the sun. As none of them would comply with this condition, they were conducted to the place of execution and the executioners applied themselves to the task of slaying these martyrs. Symeon exhorted them to constancy and reasoned concerning death, and the resurrection, and piety, and showed them from the Sacred Scriptures that a death like theirs is true life, whereas to live and through fear to deny God is as truly death. He told them, too, that even if no one were to slay them, death would inevitably overtake them, for our death is a natural consequence of our birth, and that after this short and transitory life, an account must be rendered of our actions, after which we enter upon another life wherein virtue receives eternal rewards and vice is visited with endless punishment. He likewise told them that the most glorious of good actions is to die for the cause of God.

The martyrs gladly listened to this discourse of Symeon's and went forward with alacrity to meet their death. After the execution of three hundred martyrs, Symeon himself was slain, and Abdechalaas and Ananias, two presbyters of his own church who had been his fellow-prisoners, suffered with him.

Book II, Chapter 11

Pusicius, the superintendant of the king's artisans, was present at the execution. Perceiving that Ananias trembled as the necessary preparations for his death were being made, he said to him, "Oh, old man, close your eyes and be of good courage, for you will soon behold the light of Christ."

No sooner had he uttered these words than he was arrested and conducted before the king, and as he frankly avowed himself a Christian and spoke with great boldness concerning the truth of his religion and the innocence of the martyrs, he was condemned to a most extraordinary and cruel death. The executioners pierced the muscles of his neck in such a manner as to extract his tongue. At the same time his daughter who had devoted herself to a life of holy virginity was arraigned and executed.

The following year, on the day on which the Passion of Christ was commemorated and when preparations were being made for the celebration of the festival commemorative of His Resurrection from the dead, Sapor issued a most cruel edict throughout Persia, condemning to death all those who should confess themselves to be Christians. And it is said that an immense number of Christians suffered by the sword.

The Magi sought diligently in the cities and villages for those who had concealed themselves, and many voluntarily surrendered themselves, lest they should appear by their silence to deny Christ. Of the Christians who were thus unsparingly sacrificed, many who were attached to the palace were slain, and amongst these was Azadas, a eunuch, who was especially beloved by the king. On hearing of his death Sapor was overwhelmed with grief and put a stop to the indiscriminate slaughter of the Christians, and he directed that the teachers of religion should alone be slain.

Book II, Chapter 12

About the same period, the queen was attacked with a disease and Tarbula, the sister of Symeon the bishop, a holy virgin, was arrested, as likewise her sister who was a widow and had abjured a second marriage and her servant who, like her, had devoted herself to a religious life. The cause of their arrest was the calumny of the Jews who reported that they had injured the queen by their enchantments in revenge for the death of Symeon. As invalids easily give credit to the most frightful representations, the queen believed the calumny and especially because it emanated from the Jews, for she had great confidence in their veracity and in their attachment for herself—she had embraced their sentiments, and lived in the observance of the Jewish rites.

The Magi having seized Tarbula and her companions, condemned them to death and after having sawn them asunder, fastened them up to posts, advising the queen to pass through the place of execution that the charm might be dissolved and the disease removed. It is said that Tarbula was extremely beautiful and that one of the Magi having become deeply enamored with her, sent some money secretly to her and promised to save her and her companions if she would accede to his desires. But instead of listening to his proposals, she rebuked his licentiousness and joyfully prepared for death, for she preferred to die rather than to lose her virginity.

As it was ordained by the edict of Sapor which we mentioned above that the Christians should not be slaughtered indiscriminately, but that the priests and teachers of religion should be slain, the Magi and Archmagi traversed the whole country of Persia in search of the bishops and presbyters. They sought them especially in the country of the Adiabenians, a part of the Persian dominions in which many Christians were located.

Book II, Chapter 13

About this period they arrested Acepsimus the bishop and many of his clergy. After having taken counsel together, they despoiled the clergy and then dismissed them. James, however, who was one of the presbyters, voluntarily followed Acepsimus, obtained permission from the Magi to share his prison, and joyfully ministered to him and dressed his wounds, for the Magi had cruelly scourged him in order to compel him to worship the sun and on his refusal to do so had remanded him to prison. Two priests, named Aithalas and James, and two deacons, by name Azadanus and Abdiesus, were castigated and imprisoned in the same manner by the Magi on account of their adherence to the doctrines of Christ.

After a long time had elapsed, the great Arch-magi inquired of the king what was his pleasure concerning them, and having received permission to deal with them as he pleased unless they would consent to worship the sun, he made known this decision of Sapor's to the prisoners. They replied that they would never betray the cause of Christ nor worship the sun, and were immediately subjected to the most excruciating tortures. Acepsimus persevered in the manly confession of his faith till death put an end to his torments. Certain Armenians whom the

Persians retained as hostages secretly carried away his body and buried it. The other prisoners were severely scourged but did not expire beneath the blows, and as they would not renounce their sentiments, were again consigned to prison. Aithalas was one of those who experienced this treatment. Both his arms were broken when preparations were being made for the scourging, and he afterwards lost the use of his hands so completely that he was obliged to depend upon others to convey the food to his mouth.

Subsequently, a multitude of presbyters, deacons, monks, holy virgins, ministers of the church, and laborers in word and doctrine, terminated their lives by martyrdom. The following are the names of the bishops, so far as I have been able to ascertain: Barbasymes, Paul, Gadiabes, Sabinus, Mareas, Mocius, John, Hormisdas, Papas, James, Romas, Maares, Agas, Bochres, Abdas, Abdiesus, John, Abraham, Agdelas, Sapor, Isaac, and Dausas. The latter had been made prisoner by the Persians and brought from a place named Zabdæus. He died about this time in defense of the Christian doctrine and Mareabdes, a chorepiscopus and about two hundred and fifty of his clergy, who had also been captured by the Persians, suffered with him.

Book II, Chapter 14

About this period Milles suffered martyrdom. He originally served the Persians in a military capacity, but afterwards abandoned that vocation in order to embrace the apostolical mode of life. It is related that he was ordained bishop over a Persian city where he underwent a variety of sufferings, and that failing in his efforts to convert the inhabitants to Christianity, he uttered imprecations against the city and departed.

Not long after, some of the principal citizens incurred the anger of the king, and an army with three hundred elephants was sent against them. The city was utterly demolished, and corn was sown on its site. Milles, taking with him nothing but the holy Book of the Gospels, repaired to Jerusalem to worship. Thence he proceeded to Egypt in order to see the monks. The extraordinary and admirable works which he accomplished are attested by the Syrians, who have written an account of his life and actions.

For my own part, I think that I have said enough of him and of the other martyrs who suffered in Persia during the reign of Sapor. It would be difficult to relate in detail every circumstance respecting them, such as their names, their country, the mode of their martyrdom, and the species of torture to which they were subjected. I shall briefly state that the number of men and women whose names have been ascertained and who were martyred at this period, has been computed to be upwards of sixteen thousand, while the multitude of martyrs whose names are unknown was so great that the Persians, the Syrians, and the inhabitants of Edessa, have failed in all their efforts to compute the number.[4]

NOTES

1. This famous passage may be found in the *Life of the Blessed Emperor Constantine*, Book I, Chapter 28 by Eusebius Pamphilus who claims that Constantine "declared it to the writer of this history, when he was honored with his acquaintance and society, and confirmed the statement with an oath."
2. This and more horrific detail of the death of Galerius may be found in the work of Lactantius entitled, *On the Manner in Which the Persecutors Died*, Chapter 33, which was written less than 20 years after the events described.
3. Sozomen's estimate of the death-toll of the Persian persecution may be found in Book II, Chapter 14 of his *Ecclesiastical History*.
4. These passages from Sozomen may all be found in the above mentioned *Ecclesiastical History*.

Chapter 21

Martyrs during the Reign of Julian the Apostate

Following the death of Constantine, the growth of Christianity continued, slowed only by the occasional outbreaks of rancorous debate and disunity among the bishops over matters of doctrine. Though not yet the official religion of the Roman Empire, by the end of the reign of Constantine's son, Constantius II, Christianity was dominant throughout most of the provinces.

In AD 360, Constantine's nephew Julian was proclaimed emperor in the West. Though raised as a Christian, Julian rejected the faith and with the unholy zeal of the fallen-away he was "convinced that the fabrication of the Galilæans is a fiction of men composed by wickedness."[1]

An open and staunch opponent of Christianity, Julian sought to reaffirm paganism as the de facto religion of the Roman Empire. In his methods, however, he was far more subtle than Diocletian, Valerian, Decius or any of the previous persecuting emperors. He did not declare a new persecution and even forbade open attacks on the persons or property of Christians. Instead, he attempted to strip Christians of their honors and positions in Roman society. He demanded that demolished pagan temples be rebuilt at Christian expense, forbade Christians to participate in traditional classical education, and attempted to reform the pagan priesthood and cults which had fallen into disrepute.

I AM A CHRISTIAN

However, with such an ardent foe of Christianity on the throne, many pagans throughout the empire assumed that it was only a matter of time before outright attacks on Christians would resume. Taking matters into their own hands, Roman pagans in many cities assaulted their Christian neighbors with a ferocity that rivaled that of the Great Persecution sixty years before.

For a few records of these horrific events, we turn again to the Ecclesiastical History *of Sozomen, written about 80 years later. The three episodes described here happened in Roman Palestine, Lebanon and Syria—regions that Sozomen would have known intimately as he had been raised near Gaza and schooled in Berytus, modern-day Beirut.*

MARTYRDOM ACCOUNTS FROM THE REIGN OF JULIAN THE APOSTATE FROM THE *ECCLESIASTICAL HISTORY* OF SOZOMEN

Book V, Chapter IV

...It was not from any feeling of compassion towards the Christians that [Julian the Apostate] treated them at first with greater humanity than had been evinced by former persecutors, but because he had discovered that the pagans had derived no advantage from their cruelty, while Christianity had been honored by the fortitude of those who died in defense of the faith. It was simply from envy of their glory, that instead of employing fire and the sword against them like former persecutors, and instead of casting them into the sea or burying them alive in order to compel them to renounce their sentiments, he had recourse to argument and persuasion and sought by these means to seduce them to paganism. And he expected to gain his ends more easily by abandoning all violent measures and by the manifestation of unexpected benevolence.

Book V, Chapter IX

I deem it right to relate some particulars concerning the death of the three brethren, Eusebius, Nestabis, and Zeno. The inhabitants of Gaza, being inflamed with rage against them, dragged them from their house in which they had concealed themselves and cast them into prison, after having beaten them with unexampled cruelty. They then assembled in the theater and cried out loudly against them, declaring that they had committed sacrilege in their temple and had used the power with which they were formerly invested to the injury and destruction of paganism. By these declamations the general excitement was increased to such a pitch that they ran to the prison and with unparalleled fury drew forth their victims and dashed them on the ground. And in this position, sometimes with the face and sometimes with the back upon the ground, the victims were dragged through the streets of the city and were afterwards stoned and beaten. I have been told that even women quitted their work to add to their sufferings by personal inflictions, and that the cooks left their employment to pour boiling water on them and to wound them with their culinary utensils.

When the martyrs had been literally torn to pieces and their brains scattered on the ground, their bodies were dragged out of the city and flung on the spot generally used as a receptacle for the bodies of beasts. Then a large fire was lighted, and their bones mixed with those of asses and camels, so that it might be difficult to distinguish them. But they were not long concealed, for a Christian woman who was an inhabitant though not a native of the city, collected the bones at night by the inspiration of God and conveyed them in a vessel to Zeno, their cousin, even as God had commanded her in a dream. For she was previously unacquainted with Zeno, and he had narrowly escaped being arrested, but he had effected his escape while the people were occupied in the murder of his cousins and had fled to Anthedona, a maritime city about twenty stadia from Gaza, wholly addicted to superstition and idolatry. When the inhabitants of this city discovered that he was a Christian, they beat him violently, and drove him away. He then fled to Gaza and concealed himself, and here the woman found him and gave him the remains. He kept them carefully in his house until the reign of Theodosius, when he was ordained bishop and he erected a church beyond the walls of the city and deposited the bones on the altar, near those of Nestor the Confessor.

Nestor had been on terms of intimacy with his cousins, and was seized with them by the people of Gaza, scourged, and imprisoned. But those who dragged him through the city were affected by his personal beauty and struck with compassion, they cast him, before he was quite dead, out of the city. Some persons found him and carried him to the house of Zeno, where he expired during the dressing of his wounds.

Book V, Chapter X

The inhabitants of Gaza and of Alexandria were not the only citizens who exercised such atrocities against the Christians as those I have described. The inhabitants of Heliopolis, near Mount Libanus, and of Arethusa in Syria, perpetrated deeds of still greater cruelty. The former were guilty of an act of barbarity which could scarcely be credited had it not been corroborated by the testimony of those who witnessed it. They stripped the holy virgins, who had never been looked upon by the multitude, of their garments and exposed them in a state of nudity, as public objects of insult and derision. After numerous other inflictions, they shaved them, ripped them open, and placed inside them the food usually given to pigs, and the animals thus devoured these human entrails in conjunction with their ordinary food. I am convinced that the citizens perpetrated this barbarity against the holy virgins from motives of revenge, on account of the abolition of the ancient custom of yielding up virgins to prostitution, when on the eve of marriage to those to whom they had been betrothed. This custom was prohibited by a law enacted by Constantine, after he had destroyed the temple of Venus at Heliopolis and erected a church upon its ruins.

Mark, bishop of Arethusa, an aged and virtuous prelate, was put to a very cruel death by the inhabitants of that city who had long entertained inimical feelings against him because he had, during the reign of Constantine, resorted to violence rather than to persuasion in his attempts to lead them from paganism to

Christianity and had demolished a costly and magnificent temple. On the accession of Julian, an edict was issued commanding the bishop either to rebuild the temple or to defray the expenses of its re-erection. Perceiving that the people had risen up against him and reflecting that he had no means to pay for the re-erection of the temple, and that such an act was not lawful for a Christian and still less for a bishop, he fled from the city.

On hearing, however, that many were suffering on his account, that some were dragged before the tribunals and others tortured, he returned and offered to suffer whatever the multitude might choose to inflict upon him. The people, instead of admiring this noble deed, conceived that he was actuated by contempt towards them and rushed upon him, dragged him through the streets and covered him with blows. People of each sex and of all ages joined with alacrity and fury in this atrocious proceeding. Some pierced his ears. The young men who frequented the schools made game of him, throwing him from one to the other, and they lacerated him cruelly with their knives.

When his whole body was covered with wounds, they anointed him with honey and, placing him in a basket of rushes, raised him up on an eminence. It is said that while he was in this position, and suffering from the attacks of bees and wasps, he told the inhabitants of Arethusa that he was raised up above them, and could look down upon them below him, and that this reminded him of the difference that would exist between them in the life to come. It is also related that the prefect who, although a pagan, was held in such estimation that his memory is still honored in that country, admired the fortitude of Mark and boldly uttered reproaches against the emperor for allowing himself to be vanquished by an old man, exposed to innumerable tortures, and he added that such proceedings reflected ridicule on the emperor, while the names of the persecuted were at the same time rendered illustrious. Thus did Mark endure all the torments inflicted upon him by the inhabitants of Gaza with such unshaken fortitude that even the pagans were struck with admiration.[2]

I AM A CHRISTIAN

NOTES

1. This quote is taken from Julian's polemic entitled *Against the Galileans* which may be found in *The Works of the Emperor Julian*, Volume III by Wilmer Cave Wright.
2. All excerpts from Sozomen are taken from *The Ecclesiastical History of Sozomen* which is Volume 12 of the Christian Roman Empire series.

Epilogue

Julian reigned alone as emperor for about eighteen months. While on a campaign in Persia, he was hit in the abdomen by a lance during an ambush. The Christian historian Theodoret, writing about 80 years after the event, claimed that upon receiving the wound, Julian filled his hands with blood, flung it into the air and cried out, "Thou hast conquered, O Galilean!"[1] The identity of Julian's attacker has been disputed since that day with some ancient sources claiming that a Persian or Arab had slain the emperor, others saying that a Christian Roman soldier had done it, and still others saying that a spiritual being of some sort had done the deed.

With Julian's death in AD 363, the era of pagan Roman persecution of Christians ended forever. A mere 17 years later, Christianity was declared the official religion of the Roman Empire by the emperors Theodosius the Great, Gratian and Valentinian II. Specifically named in this edict were the Patriarch Peter of Alexandria, successor of the great Saint Athanasius, and Pope Damasus I of Rome, who restored the catacombs of the ancient martyrs in Rome. Several metrical epitaphs written by Pope Damasus for display beside the tombs of the martyrs may be found in the following appendix.

NOTE

1. This quote may be found in Theodoret's *Ecclesiastical History* as translated by Blomfield Jackson in *A Select Library of Nicene and Post-Nicene Fathers of the Christian Church, Second Series, Volume III*.

Appendix

The Epitaphs of Pope Damasus

The following translations and explanatory notes are taken from the book Christian Inscriptions by H. P. V. Nunn (1920). The text has been edited for use in this book.

Pope Damasus was Bishop of Rome from AD 366–384. He is chiefly remarkable for the care he took to make the graves of the martyrs accessible, and for the inscriptions which he composed in their honor and had engraved in marble and placed near their tombs. His father was registrar of the Church of Rome, and subsequently a Deacon and a Bishop (see his epitaph below). In spite of the fact that he was the official guardian of the archives of the Church relating amongst other things to the acts of the martyrs, his son Damasus was often compelled to rely on tradition and hearsay evidence in compiling his poems in honor of the martyrs. This seems to have been due to the complete destruction of the records of the Roman Church during the persecution of Diocletian, and is important in relation to Church history, because it explains why we know so little of the Church in Rome before the time of Constantine, and why the existing acts of the martyrs are often so fabulous and unreliable. They were composed from tradition at a later date.

The epitaph of Damasus himself is given first, and then one that he set up in the church which he built on the site of the old registry of the Roman church where his father had lived — the church now called Saint Lorenzo in Damaso. They are followed by a selection of the epitaphs of Damasus on the martyrs, generally in chronological order. It should also *be mentioned that Damasus induced Jerome, who was at one time his secretary, to undertake the improved Latin translation of the Bible which we call the Vulgate.*

Epitaph of Damasus

> He who stilled the raging waves of the sea by walking thereon, He who makes the dying seeds of the earth to live, He who could loose for Lazarus the chains of death, and give back again to the world above her brother to his sister Martha after three days and nights. He, I believe, will make me, Damasus, arise from my ashes.

This epitaph was composed by Damasus to be placed on his own tomb in a basilica that he built on the Via Ardeatina. It was a place of pilgrimage until the eighth century, when his body was removed to the church of Saint Lorenzo in Damaso within the walls to protect it from the Lombards.

Epitaph of the Father of Damasus (Antonius?)

> Hence my father advanced from keeper of the records to reader, and from reader to deacon and bishop, since he was advanced by his ever-increasing merits. When I was preferred hence, Christ, who possesses the supreme power, wished to grant me the honors of the Apostolic Throne.
> I confess that I wished to build a new hall for the archives and to add columns thereto on the right and on the left, which might keep the name of Damasus as their own throughout the ages.

Epitaph of Damasus on a niche which held the bodies of Saints Peter and Paul in the catacombs

> Here, you must know, the saints dwelt aforetime. Their names, if you ask, were Peter and Paul. The East sent the disciples, as

we gladly admit. On account of the merit of their blood—and having followed Christ through the stars, they sought the ethereal havens and the realms of the just—Rome rather deserved to defend her citizens. Let Damasus thus recall your praises, ye new constellations.

This inscription was set up in the crypt behind the present Church of Saint Sebastian, formerly called the Basilica of the Apostles, on the Appian Way, to which the bodies of Saints Peter and Paul were removed from their tombs on the Vatican and the Ostian Way in AD 258, to preserve them from desecration during the persecution of Valerian.

The allusion to "disciples from the east" seems to refer to a story mentioned in the Acta Petri et Pauli *and referred to by Gregory the Great, that certain men came from the east and endeavored to remove the bodies of the Apostles from Rome on the ground that they were citizens of the East. Damasus says that they had become citizens of Rome by their death in that city, and that Rome, therefore, deserved to retain their bodies.*

Damasus's epitaph for Saints Nereus and Achilleus

They had given their names for military service, and together fulfilled their cruel office, paying heed to the commands of the tyrant, ready to obey his orders at the prompting of fear. Strange but true is the tale—suddenly they laid aside their fury, they turn and fly, they abandon the impious camp of their leader, they throw away their shields, their decorations, and their blood-stained weapons and, having witnessed a good confession, they rejoice to carry the trophies of Christ. Believe on the word of Damasus what the glory of Christ can bring to pass.

The only trustworthy tradition that has come down to us about these martyrs is contained in this epitaph. They seem to have been members of the Prætorian Guard under Nero or Domitian, and to have carried out his cruel orders against the Christians. They were suddenly converted, probably as was often the case by the fortitude of their victims. Their

Acts, which are late in date, relate that they were chamberlains of Flavia Domitilla, the Christian niece of Vespasian. They followed her to exile in Pontia, and were put to death with her in Terracina, perhaps under Trajan. Their bodies were brought to Rome and buried in the cemetery of Domitilla, where a church was built over their tomb after the time of Constantine. De Rossi discovered the ruins of this church in 1873, together with a bas-relief on a column, representing the execution of Achilleus by decapitation, and also fragments of this inscription. For the name Nereus, compare Romans 16:15.

Regarding this Domitilla, the following passage from the pagan historian Cassius Dio is instructive:

> And the same year Domitian slew, along with many others, Flavius Clemens the consul, although he was a cousin and had to wife Flavia Domitilla, who was also a relative of the emperor's. The charge brought against them both was that of atheism, a charge on which many others who drifted into Jewish ways were condemned. Some of these were put to death, and the rest were at least deprived of their property. Domitilla was merely banished to Pandateria. But Glabrio, who had been Trajan's colleague in the consulship, was put to death having been accused of the same crimes as most of the others and, in particular, of fighting as a gladiator with wild beasts. Indeed, his prowess in the arena was the chief cause of the emperor's anger against him, an anger prompted by jealousy. For in Glabrio's consulship Domitian had summoned him to his Alban estate to attend the festival called the Juvenalia and had imposed on him the task of killing a large lion. And Glabrio not only had escaped all injury but had despatched the lion with most accurate aim."[2]

Returning to the epitaphs of Damasus and turning now to the martyrs' tombs, the inscription which stood in the papal crypt of Saint Callixtus strikes, as it were, the keynote of the whole series. Those mentioned may include Pope Saint Sixtus and Saint Laurence.

The Epitaphs of Pope Damasus

Epitaph on the Papal crypt of Saint Callixtus

If thou seekest them, here lies in little space a throng of holy ones. Their honored sepulchers hold the bodies of the saints, but the realms of heaven have rapt away their lofty spirits. Here are the comrades of Sixtus (the martyred pope), who wrested victory from the enemy. Here the band of our leaders who serve the altars of Christ. Here is laid the priest who lived long days in peace. Here are the confessors of Christ who Greece sent forth. Here are young men and boys, old men and children, whose will it was to preserve their virgin purity. I confess that I, Damasus, would fain have laid my limbs here, but I feared to trouble the holy ashes of the saints.

One of the most beautiful of the epitaphs is that of the youthful martyr Gordianus, buried between the Via Labicana and Via Latina:

Epitaph of Gordianus, Martyr

You who look upon this grave, perfected with so great a labor, cease to wonder: it is less wondrous than the martyr it enshrines. He was a boy in age, a victory in his youthful years, in a little space triumphed, ripe for glory. He stained cruel weapons with his innocent blood: his murderer thirstily drank up the blood of the tender prey. Thus victorious he sought a supernal kingdom and from his heavenly dwelling visits us who enjoy peace. His name is Gordianus, whom the palm of Christ crowned. The priest Vincentius adorned and repaired the tomb at his own expense, enclosing the chest and the blessed ashes in marble.

Another well-known inscription is that of Tiburtius:

Tiburtius, on the Via Tiburtina

At the time when the sword was piercing the heart of our holy mother (the Church), this glorious martyr, despising the prince of this world, sought, blessed one, with Christ as companion, the heights of heaven. Here (at the tomb) forever shall be holy honor and praise to thee. O gentle Tiburtius, dear to God, I pray thee cherish Damasus.

Next, is an inscription dedicated to the matron Felicitas who was martyred with her seven sons during the reign of Marcus Aurelius:

Epitaph of Felicitas

Learn what merit to be smitten for a king affords: a woman feared not the sword, she perished with her sons. Having confessed Christ, she deserved a name throughout all ages.

The second and third sons of Felicitas were buried in the cemetery of Priscilla on the Via Salaria, where the Basilica of Sylvester was afterwards built. Damasus left the following epitaph to honor them:

Epitaph of Felix and Philippus

He who believes that God was born and suffered and sought again His Father's throne and that He will come again from the skies, that on his return, He may judge the living and also the dead, sees, if he follows the rewards of Christ, that the inner court of heaven lies open to the holy martyrs.

Felix and Philippus, the worshippers of the Lord, equal in valor, sought hence their eternal home and the kingdom of the righteous, despising the prince of the world. Because they merited the crowns of Christ with their own blood, Damasus, a suppliant, wished to render them his vows in these lines.

Epitaph of Saint Hippolytus, Martyr

Hippolytus is said, while the commands of the tyrant pressed hard upon us, to have ever remained as a presbyter in the schism of Novatus. At the time when the sword severed the holy bowels of our mother, when, devoted to Christ, he was seeking the kingdoms of the just, and when people had asked him where they could proceed, he is said to have replied that all should follow the Catholic faith. Thus, having made his confession, he deserved to be our martyr. Damasus reports these things that he has heard. Christ proves all things.

The above is probably the epitaph of the celebrated Hippolytus whose writings against heretics have come down to us. He was buried in a splendid shrine on the Via Tiburtina which is described by Prudentius in Peristephanon XI. *Nothing better illustrates the confusion and obscurity which enveloped the history of the Roman Church owing to the destruction of records in the persecution of Diocletian than the fact that Damasus had to depend on uncertain oral tradition in writing the epitaph of this celebrated person. He was certainly a schismatic, and in open conflict with the Popes of Rome, especially with Zephyrinus and Callixtus. Some think that he was the first anti-pope. Damasus records that he was reconciled to the Church just before his death, and therefore deserves to be treated as a martyr.*

When or how he was put to death is not known. Prudentius saw a picture in his tomb representing him being torn to pieces by wild horses. Some scholars place his death during the persecution of Valerian, others maintain that he died in exile during the reign of Maximus Thrax.

Epitaph of Pope Cornelius

Behold, now that a way of descent has been made and the darkness put to flight, you see the monument of Cornelius and his consecrated mound.

The power of Damasus in his sickness has completed this work that there might be a better mode of access and that the help of the saint might be prepared for the people, and that if you prevail to pour forth prayers from a pure heart, Damasus may rise up stronger, though it is not love of the light that possesses him, but rather care for his work.

Cornelius was bishop of Rome from AD *251–253, a friend of Saint Cyprian (see Chapter 11 of the present volume). He was exiled to Civita Vecchia by Gallus, where he died. He was regarded as a martyr. It was the discovery of a fragment of his gravestone that led to the discovery of the catacomb of Callixtus and the Papal crypt in 1849.*

EPITAPH OF POPE SIXTUS II

At the time when the sword severed the holy bowels of our mother, I, the ruler, was seated here teaching the Divine laws: those come suddenly who are to seize me on my throne. Then the people gave their necks to the soldiers who were sent, but when the elder knew who wished to bear away the palm, he offered himself and his life of his own accord first of all, lest their impatient frenzy should injure anyone. Christ, who awards the prizes of life, shows the merit of the Shepherd. He Himself keeps the number of the flock.

This epitaph refers to Pope Sixtus II, Pope of Rome, AD *257–258. He was captured while preaching to the people in the cemetery of Pretextatus, which was situated in private property on the other side of the Appian Way from that of Callixtus, and he was put to death with the second edict of Valerian, which condemned all Christian clergy without trial. He was afterwards buried with four deacons who were executed with him in the Papal crypt in the catacomb of Callixtus. This inscription and the next one were placed in the crypt by Damasus.*

EPITAPH OF THE MARTYR TARSACIUS

Whosoever thou art that readest, recognize the equal merit of these two to whom Damasus the ruler sets up as memorials after they have attained their reward.
    The people of the Jews had smitten down Stephen with stones while he was calling them to higher things, Stephen who had borne away the trophy of the enemy: the faithful Levite first snatched the crown of martyrdom.

When a frenzied hand sought to do dishonor to holy Tarsacius as he was carrying the Sacrament of Christ, he preferred to be slain and to lose his life, rather than to betray the Divine limbs to mad dogs.

Above is the epitaph of Tarsacius, an acolyte, who was killed in the persecution of Valerian while carrying the sacramental elements to the cemetery of Callixtus, then confiscated and guarded by the police. He was buried with the Bishop, Saint Zephyrinus, in a chapel erected above the Papal crypt.

Epitaph of Peter and Marcellinus, Martyrs

When I was a boy your executioner made known to me thy triumphs, O Marcellinus, and thine also, O Peter. The mad butcher gave him this commandment—that he should sever your necks in the midst of the thickets in order that no one should be able to recognize your grave, and he told how you prepared your sepulcher with eager hands. Afterwards you lay hid in a white cave, and then Lucilla was caused to know by your goodness that it pleased you rather to lay your sacred limbs here.

Above is the epitaph of Peter, a priest, and Marcellinus, an exorcist, who were put to death in AD 304 in the persecution of Diocletian. It was placed in the cemetery called after them on the Via Labicana. Their names are still mentioned in the Canon of the Mass. This inscription is interesting as showing the care taken by the Roman Government during the later persecutions to prevent honor being done to the bodies of the martyrs. Even the stories of their deaths were suppressed: Damasus had to go to the executioner for details. It also illustrates the interest that Damasus took in the martyrs from an early age.

Epitaph of Marcellus, Pope of Rome

The truth-telling ruler, because he bade the lapsed weep for their crimes, became a bitter enemy to all these unhappy men.

I AM A CHRISTIAN

Hence followed rage and hate, and discord and strife, sedition and slaughter. The bonds of peace are loosed. On account of the crimes of another, who denied Christ in time of peace, he was driven from the borders of his fatherland by the savagery of the tyrant.

Damasus wishes briefly to tell these things which he had found out, that the people might know the merit of Marcellus.

Epitaph of Pope Marcellus who was elected in AD 308, after the long vacancy of the Roman See caused by the persecution of Diocletian. He established twenty-five parishes in Rome, and opened a new cemetery near the cemetery of Priscilla, where he is buried. His firm handling of those who had denied the faith during the persecution led to a revolt against his authority, and he was banished by Maxentius. He died in exile.

Epitaph for Pope Eusebius

Damasus the Bishop erected this.

Heraclius forbade the lapsed to mourn for their sins. Eusebius taught the unhappy men to weep for their crimes. The people are divided into parties as the madness grew—sedition, slaughter, war, discord, strife. Suddenly both were driven out by the cruelty of the tyrant, and since the ruler had kept the bonds of peace inviolate, he gladly endured exile under the judgment of the Lord and left the world and his life on the Trinacrian shore.

To Eusebius, bishop and martyr.

Eusebius was elected bishop of Rome after the banishment of Marcellus, and dealt as firmly as he had done with the lapsed. Heraclius was the leader of the party opposed to him, who wished the lapsed to be readmitted to the Church on easy terms. Maxentius banished both of them, and Eusebius died in exile in Sicily. He was buried in a special crypt in the cemetery of Callixtus, where an early copy of this inscription may still be seen. These last two inscriptions make known to us a chapter in Church history which is otherwise unrecorded.

The Epitaphs of Pope Damasus

See also the epitaphs by Pope Damasus of Saint Lawrence and Saint Agnes which are included beginning on pages 104 and 143 respectively of the present volume.

NOTES

1. All the epitaphs of Damasus contained in this appendix along with some of the explanatory text may be found in *Christian Inscriptions* by H. P. V. Nunn.
2. This passage from Cassius Dio is taken from his *Roman History*, Epitome of Book LXVII, as translated into English by Earnest Cary. It should be noted that the charge of "atheism" was one commonly assessed to Christians who refused to recognize the pagan pantheon.

Sources

Ambrose of Milan. H. De Romestin (transl.) 1896. *A Select Library of Nicene and Post-Nicene Fathers of the Christian Church, Volume X: Saint Ambrose*. Parker and Company: Oxford.
Apollonius. F. C. Conybeare (transl.) 1896. *The Armenian Apology and Acts of Apollonius and Other Monuments of Early Christianity, Second Edition*. Swan Sonnenschein: London.
Atteridge, A. Hilliard. 1918. "A Light on the Early Persecutions," in *America: A Catholic Review of the Week*, America Press: New York. Vol. 19, p. 308.
Augustine of Hippo. Edmund Hill (transl.) 1994. *The Works of Saint Augustine: A Translation for the 21st Century. Sermons III/8 (273-305A) On the Saints*. New City Press: New York.
Augustine of Hippo. Maria Boulding (transl.) 2003. *The Works of Saint Augustine: A Translation for the 21st Century. Expositions of the Psalms, 99-120*. New City Press: New York.
Barker, Ethel Ross. 1913. *Rome of the Pilgrims and Martyrs*. Methuen and Co.: London.
Bennett, Charles W. 1888. *Christian Archaeology*. Phillips and Hunt: New York.
Butler, Alban. 1821. *Lives of the Fathers, Martyrs and Other Principal Saints, Vol. IV*. John Murphy: London.
Cassius Dio. Earnest Cary (transl.) 1925. *Roman History*, Volume VIII. G. P. Putnam's Sons: New York.
Cyprian. "Acta Proconsularia Cypriani" in *Translations and Reprints from the Original Sources of European History*, Vol. IV. Department of History of the University of Pennsylvania: Philadelphia.
Eusebius Pamphilus. Arthur C. McGiffert (transl.) 1890. *A Select Library of Nicene and Post-Nicene Fathers of the Christian Church, Volume I: Eusebius*. Parker and Company: Oxford.
Eusebius Pamphilus. 2009. *Life of the Blessed Emperor Constantine*. Evolution Publishing: Merchantville, NJ.
Historia Augusta (anonymous). David Magie (transl.) 1921. *Historia Augusta, Volume 1*. Harvard University Press: Cambridge, MA.
Ignatius of Antioch. Alexander Roberts and James Donaldson (transl.) 1885. *Ante-Nicene Fathers, Volume 1: The Apostolic Fathers*. Christian Literature Publishing Co.: Buffalo, NY.

Jerome. Thomas P. Halton (transl.) 1999. *Saint Jerome: On Illustrious Men*. Catholic University of America Press: Washington, DC.

Julian the Apostate. Wilmer Cave Wright (transl.) 1923. *Works*. Putnam and Sons: NY.

Justin Martyr. Marcus Dods, George Reith and B. P. Pratten (transl.) 1879. *Ante-Nicene Christian Library, Volume 2: The Writings of Justin Martyr and Athenagoras*. T&T Clark: Edinburgh.

Lactantius. William Fletcher (transl.) 1871. *Ante-Nicene Christian Library, Vol. 12: The Works of Lactantius, Volume 2*. T&T Clark: Edinburgh.

Leo the Great. Charles Lett Feltoe (transl.) 1895. *A Select Library of Nicene and Post-Nicene Fathers of the Christian Church, Volume XII: Leo the Great, Gregory the Great*. Parker and Company: Oxford.

Ligouri, Alphonsus. Eugene Grimm. 1888. *Victories of the Martyrs*. Benziger Brothers: New York.

Mason, Arthur James. 1905. *The Historic Martyrs of the Primitive Church*. Longmans, Green and Co.: London.

Mathetes (Anonymous). Alexander Roberts and James Donaldson (transl.) 1885. *Ante-Nicene Fathers, Volume 1: The Apostolic Fathers*. Christian Literature Publishing Co.: Buffalo, NY.

Nunn, H. P. V. 1920. *Christian Inscriptions*. Society for Promoting Christian Knowledge: London.

Optatus. O. R. Vassall-Phillips. 1917. *The Work of Saint Optatus, Bishop of Milevis, Against the Donatists*. Longmans, Green, and Co.: London.

Origen. John Clark Smith (transl.) 1998. *Homilies on Jeremiah and 1 Kings 28*. Catholic University of America Press: Washington, DC.

Perpetua and Felicitas. R. E. Wallis (transl.) 1885. *Ante-Nicene Fathers, Volume III: Latin Christianity, Its Founder, Tertullian*. Christian Literature Publishing Co.: Buffalo, NY.

Polycarp. Alexander Roberts and James Donaldson (transl.) 1885. *Ante-Nicene Fathers, Volume 1: The Apostolic Fathers*. Christian Literature Publishing Co.: Buffalo, NY.

Pontius the Deacon. 2013. "The Life and Passion of Cyprian," in *The Complete Works of Saint Cyprian*. Evolution Publishing: Merchantville, NJ.

Prudentius. Francis St. John Thackeray (transl.) 1890. *Translations from Prudentius*. George Bell and Sons: London.

Prudentius. R. O. (transl.) 1873. "A Hymn of Prudentius" in *The Month: A Magazine and Review*, Volume 18, May-June. Simpkin, Marshall and Co.: London.

Scillitan Martyrs. A. Robinson (transl.) 1896. *Ante-Nicene Fathers, Volume 9*. Christian Literature Publishing Co.: Buffalo, NY.

Sozomen. Edward Walford (transl.) 2018. *The Ecclesiastical History of Sozomen*. Evolution Publishing: Merchantville, NJ.

Tacitus. John Jackson (transl.) 1937. *Annals*. Harvard University Press: Cambridge, MA.

Theodoret. Blomfield Jackson (transl.) 1892. *A Select Library of Nicene and Post-Nicene Fathers of the Christian Church, Second Series, Volume III: Theodoret, Jerome, Gennadius, Rufinus: Historical Writings, etc.* The Christian Literature Company: New York.

Tertullian. T. Herbert Bindley (transl.) 1914. *On the Testimony of the Soul and On the "Prescription" of Heretics*. Society for Promoting Christian Knowledge: London.

Trajan. John Delaware Lewis (transl.) 1890. *The Letters of the Younger Pliny*. Paul, Trench Trübner & Co.: London.

Index

Abdas, bishop, martyr 168
Abdechalaas, presbyter, martyr 165
Abdiesus 167–168
Abdiesus, bishop, martyr 168
Abdiesus, deacon, confessor 167–168
Abitina x, 129–133, 135, 137–138, 140
Abraham, bishop, martyr 168
Abraham, patriarch 4, 104
Acepsimus, bishop, martyr 167
Achilleus, martyr 17, 181–182
Ælius 110
Æmilianus, consul 109–112
Africa 6, 51, 55, 100, 124, 129, 139–141, 143
Agape, martyr x, 115, 117–119, 121–122
Agas, bishop, martyr 168
Agatho 117–118, 122
Agathopus 18
Agdelas, bishop, martyr 168
Agnes, martyr 143–149, 189
Aithalas, presbyter, confessor 167–168
Alce 34
Alexander, martyr 81
Alexander Severus, emperor 77
Alexandria 10, 16, 73, 75, 77–79, 81, 83, 85, 174, 177
Ambrose, Saint 103–104, 107, 143–144, 148
Ammon, martyr 82
Ammonarion, martyr 81
Ampelius, martyr 135
Ananias, presbyter, martyr 165

Anthedona 173
Antioch 4, 18–21, 23–24, 78, 83
Antonius 180
Anulinus, proconsul 129–131, 133–138, 140–141
Apollonia, martyr 79
Apollonius, martyr 43–49
Aquila 74
Aquilinus, martyr 53
Arethusa 174–175
Artaxius, martyr 64
Artemesius, secretary 117
Asia 4, 6–7, 21, 25, 31, 51
Aspasius, presbyter 65
Ater, martyr 81
Athanasius, Saint 177
Athens 46
Augurius, deacon xiii, 109, 110
Augustalis, reader 111
Augustine, Saint xiii, xiv, 109, 139–140, 142
Aurelius, soldier 110
Azadanus, deacon, confessor 167
Azadas 166

Babylas 112
Barbasymes, bishop, martyr 168
Basilides, martyr 73–75
Bassus, consul 95, 109
Berytus (Beirut) 172
Besas, martyr 81
Bithynia 6, 17

193

Bochres, bishop, martyr 168
Bos 127
Britain 150, 159

Caius 36
Calahorra 149, 152, 158
Callixtus, Pope 182–183, 185–188
Candidianus, Macrobius, procurator 101
Cappadocia 6, 40
Carosus, subdeacon 125–127
Carthage 51–52, 55, 93–94, 96, 100, 109, 130, 132
Carus, emperor 116
Casia 117–118, 122
Cassander 117
Cassius Dio 18, 24, 182, 189
Catullinus, subdeacon 125–126
Celedonius, martyr 149, 152
Ceres 68
Chæremon, martyr 82
Charites, martyr 38, 41
Charito, martyr 39
Chariton, martyr 38–39, 41
Chionia, Saint x, 115, 117–119, 122
Cirta 124, 129
Cittinus, martyr 52–53
Civita Vecchia 186
Claudianus 52
Clemens, Flavius 17, 149, 182
Clement of Alexandria, Saint 10, 16
Clopas 10–11
Coddeo 127
Commodus, emperor 43–45
Constantine the Great, emperor 124, 140, 150, 159–160, 169, 171, 174, 179, 182
Constantius I, emperor 116, 150, 159
Constantius II, emperor 171
Corinth 7, 36
Cornelius, pope 185–186
Crescens 37
Crispina, martyr 129, 139–142
Crocus 18
Ctesiphon 115, 161
Curubis (see *Curubitana*)
Curubitana 95
Cyprian, Saint 93–102, 186

Dalmatia 116
Damasus, Pope 103–104, 143–144, 148, 177, 179–189
Dativus, martyr 130–133
Dausas 168
Dausas, bishop, martyr 168
Decius, emperor 73, 77–78, 85–86, 93–94, 116, 171
Deusatelium 125
de Ligouri, Alphonsus, Saint 139, 142
Dinocrates 55, 61, 62, 71
Diocletian, emperor x, 115–117, 122–124, 149–150, 159–160, 171, 179, 185, 187–188
Diogenes, Aurelius 77–78
Diognetus 13, 16
Dionysia, martyr 81
Dionysius, Saint 78, 83
Dioscorus, confessor 81
Domitian, emperor 17, 19, 181–182
Domitilla, Flavia 17, 182
Donata, martyr 52–53
Donatus 110
Dulcetius, governor 117–121

Ebaracum (York) 159
Edessa 115, 169
Edusius 125–126
Elijah, prophet 105
Elisha, prophet 105
Emerita (Mérida) 149
Emeritus, martyr 133–135
Emeterius, martyr 149, 152
Ephesus 7
Epidamnus 22
Epimachus, martyr 81
Epirus 22
Euelpistus, martyr 39–40
Eugenius 126
Eulalia, martyr 149–150
Eulogius, deacon xiii, 109–110
Eunous, Cronion, martyr 80
Eusebius, martyr 172
Eusebius, Pope 188
Eusebius Pamphilus 6, 10–11, 16, 25, 43, 76, 78, 83, 123, 128, 159, 169
Euticius 127
Eutychia 117–119, 122

Index

Evarestus 35
Exuperius, Saint 85, 90

Fabian, bishop of Antioch 78, 83
Fabian, Pope 85
Felicitas, martyr in Carthage 55–59, 61, 63, 65–67, 69, 71
Felicitas, martyr in Rome 184
Felix, a Christian in Tarragona 111
Felix, martyr in Rome 184
Felix, Munatius, curator of Cirta 124–127
Felix, Octavius, martyr 130
Felix, sculptor 127
Felix of Abitina, martyr 135–136
Felix of Abitina (the younger), martyr 136
Felix of Scillitum, martyr 53
Fortunatian 137
Fructuosus, grave digger 125
Fructuosus, Saint xiii, xiv, 109–113

Gadiabes, bishop, martyr 168
Galatia 6
Galerius, emperor x, 116–117, 123–124, 150, 156, 159–160, 169
Galerius Maximus, proconsul 94–96, 98, 102
Gallienus, emperor 94–95, 99, 109, 115
Gallus, Trebonius 186
Gaul 85, 150
Gaza 172–175
Generosa, martyr 53
Germanicus, martyr 27
Geta, emperor 62
Glabrio 17, 182
Gordianus, martyr 183
Gratian, emperor 177
Gratus, consul 85–86
Greece 7, 183
Gregory of Tours 85
Gregory the Great, pope 107, 181

Hadrian, emperor 9
Hegesippus 11, 16
Helena, Saint 150
Heliopolis 174
Helius, deacon 125
Heracles 46
Heraclides, martyr 74

Heraclius 188
Herais, martyr 74
Hero, martyr 74
Herod, Irenarch of Smyrna 28–29, 34–35
Herod Agrippa, king 10
Heron, martyr 81
Hierax, martyr 39, 40
Hilarian, martyr 137
Hilarianus, procurator 60–61, 68
Hilarius, Saint 89
Hippolytus, martyr 184, 185
Hormisdas, bishop, martyr 168

Iconium 40
Ignatius of Antioch, saint 17–25
Illyricum 6
Ingenuus, martyr 82
Irenæus of Lyons 36
Irene, martyr x, 115, 117–122
Isaac, bishop, martyr 168
Isaiah, prophet 12, 16
Ischyrion, martyr 82
Isidore, martyr 81

James, bishop, martyr 168
James, presbyter, confessor 167
James the Greater, Saint 5, 9–10
James the Less (James the Just), Saint 5, 10–13
Januaria, martyr 53
Januarius, grave digger 125
Jeremiah, prophet 13, 75
Jerome, Saint 43, 49, 180
Jerusalem 4, 6, 10, 168
Jesus the Christ xiii, xiv, 3–5, 9–14, 20, 24, 26, 32–33, 35–36, 38, 40–41, 57, 59, 70, 91, 106, 113, 119–120, 131, 140, 142, 157
Jews 6, 12–14, 31–32, 34, 161–162, 166, 186
Jocundus, martyr 64
John, bishop, martyr 168
John the Evangelist, Saint xiv, 3, 5, 7, 9–10, 15, 17–19, 21, 25, 91
Joseph, Saint 11
Judæa 47
Julian, martyr 80, 81
Julian, presbyter 101

I AM A CHRISTIAN

Julian, subdeacon 101
Julian the Apostate, emperor 171–173, 175–177
Junius, notary 125, 126
Justin Martyr, Saint 36–41

Lactantius 93, 102, 115–116, 122, 143, 148, 160, 169
Lætantius, martyr 53
Lawrence, deacon, martyr 103–107, 189
Leonides 73
Leo the Great, Pope 103, 106–107
Liberianus, martyr 38, 40–41
Lucilla 187
Luke, Saint xiv, 3

Maares, bishop, martyr 168
Macedonia 7, 22, 117
Magi 161–162, 164, 166–167
Mammæa, Julia 77
Marcellinus, exorcist, martyr 187
Marcellus, Pope 187–188
Marcion 25
Marcuclius, subdeacon 125–126
Marcus, disciple of Polycarp 35
Marcus Aurelius, emperor 25, 37, 184
Mareabdes, chorepiscopus, martyr 168
Mareas, bishop, martyr 168
Mark, bishop, confessor 174–175
Mark, Saint xiv
Mars, deacon 125
Martinus 39
Mary, martyr 138
Mary, wife of Clopas 10
Matthew, Saint xiv, 9, 16, 18, 91, 107
Mauar, martyr 81
Maxentius, usurper 140, 159, 188
Maximian, emperor 116, 122, 124, 143, 150, 159
Maximian, martyr 136
Maximus, soldier 110
Maximus Thrax, emperor 185
Memorius, priest 125
Meraclus 125
Meraclus, grave digger 125
Mercuria, martyr 81
Metras, martyr 79
Migginis 125

Migginis, grave digger 125
Milan 103, 143–144, 148, 160
Milles, martyr 168
Minerva 146
Mocius, bishop, martyr 168
Montanus, priest 125
Mydonius 112

Nartzalus, martyr 52–53
Neapolis 22
Nemesion, martyr 82
Nereus, martyr 17, 181–182
Nero, Roman Emperor 6, 15, 17, 181
Nestabis, martyr 172
Nestor, martyr 174
Nicanor, deacon 3
Nicetes 29, 34
Nicolas, deacon 4
Nicomedia 116
Nilopolis 82
Novatus 185
Numerian, emperor 116
Numidia 124

Optatus, bishop 65
Orestes 105
Origen 6, 15, 73–75, 77
Ostia 9

Pæon, martyr 38–41
Palestine 161, 172
Pandateria 17, 182
Pannonia 150
Papas, bishop, martyr 168
Parmenas, deacon 3
Parthians 18, 20
Paternus, Aspasius, proconsul 95
Patmos 17
Paul, bishop, martyr 168
Paul, bishop of Cirta 124–125
Paul, saint 5–10, 21–22, 53, 79, 180–181
Perennius, prefect of Rome 44
Perpetua, Vivia, martyr 55–57, 59, 61, 63, 64–71
Persia 116, 160–161, 166–167, 169, 177
Peter, patriarch of Alexandria 177
Peter, priest of Rome, martyr 187
Peter, Saint 5–8, 104, 157, 180–181

Index

Pharisees 12
Philip, deacon 3
Philippa 117–118, 122
Philippi 7, 22
Philippus, martyr 184
Philip the Asiarch 31
Philip the Trallian 35
Philo 18
Philomelium 25
Pionius 36
Plato 37, 49
Pliny the Younger 17, 24
Plutarch, martyr 74
Pollentius 110
Polycarp 21, 25–37
Pomponius, deacon 58, 61–62
Pontia 182
Pontius, deacon 94, 96, 99
Pontius Pilate 20
Pontus 6
Portus 23
Potamiena, martyr 73, 75
Præsens 52
Pretextatus 186
Priscilla 184, 188
Prochorus, deacon 3
Projectus 127
Prudentius 7, 16, 109, 143, 146, 148–149, 150–153, 155–158, 185
Ptolemy, martyr 82
Pudens 62, 69–70
Purgatory 55, 71, 75
Pusicius, martyr 165
Puteoli 22
Pylades 105

Quadratus, Statius, proconsul 25, 35
Quinta, martyr 79
Quintus, apostate 27
Quintus, confessor 136
Quintus, martyr 64
Quirinus, martyr 150, 156

Ravenna 139
Rechab 13
Revocatus, martyr 55, 57, 68
Rogatian, martyr 136
Rogatianus 110

Romas, bishop, martyr 168
Rome 6–7, 9, 15, 18, 20–23, 25, 37–39, 41, 44, 51, 103, 109, 113, 140, 143, 145–147, 149, 159, 177, 179, 181–182, 185–188
Rusticus, a catechumen 69
Rusticus, Junius, prefect of Rome 37–41

Sabinus, bishop, martyr 168
Salutaria 96
Samaria 37
Sapor, bishop, martyr 168
Sapor I, king of Persia 115
Sapor II, king of Persia 160–164, 166–167, 169
Sarapion, martyr 79
Satabos 78
Saturninus, African martyr 55, 57, 64, 68
Saturninus, grave digger 125
Saturninus, priest, martyr 130–137
Saturninus, Vigellius, proconsul 51–53
Saturninus of Toulouse, martyr 85–89, 91
Saturui 96
Saturus, martyr 55, 59, 64, 66–70
Savus (Sava) River 157
Scillium 51
Scythians 19
Secunda, martyr 52–53
Secundulus, martyr 57, 66
Seleucia 21, 161
Septimius 55–56, 70, 73, 77
Serenus, martyr 74
Sescia (Sisak) 150, 156
Sexti 96
Sicily 188
Silvanus, subdeacon 125–127
Silvius, bishop of Toulouse 89
Sixtus II, Pope 93, 103–104, 182–183, 186
Smyrna 21–22, 25, 31, 33, 35–36
Socrates, philosopher 46
Socrates, transcriber of the martyrdom of Polycarp 36
Sol Invictus 150
Sozomen, Hermias 161, 169, 172, 176
Spain 109, 149, 152, 158
Speratus, martyr 52–53
Stephen, Saint 3–5, 104, 186

Symeon, bishop of Ctesiphon, martyr 161–163, 164–166
Syria 172, 174
Syros, Aurelius 78

Tacitus 15–16
Tarbula, martyr 166
Tarragona 109
Tarsacius, martyr 186–187
Terracina 182
Tertius, deacon 58
Tertullian 6, 16, 55–56, 71, 73, 85, 91
Testucius 110
Thagara 139–140
Thelica, martyr 130–133
Theodoret 177
Theodosius the Great, emperor 173, 177
Theophilus, martyr 82
Theophorus (see *Ignatius of Antioch*)
Thessalonica 117
Tiber River 7–9
Tiburtius, martyr 183–184
Timinianus, Minucius, proconsul 60
Timon, deacon 3
Timothy, Saint 6
Toulouse 85–86, 89
Trajan, emperor 17–20, 24, 182

Troas 22
Tuscus, consul 95

Usthazanes, martyr 162–164

Valentinian II, emperor 177
Valerian, emperor 85, 93–95, 99, 103, 109, 115–116, 171, 181, 185–187
Venerea 96
Venus 174
Vespasian, emperor 13, 182
Vestia, martyr 52–53
Veturius, martyr 53
Victor, grave digger 125
Victor, priest 125
Victoria, martyr 132, 137
Victorinus 127
Victor of Aufidus 125
Victor the Gramarian 127
Vincentius 183

Zabdæus 168
Zebedee 9
Zeno, martyr 172–174
Zenon, martyr 82
Zephyrinus, pope 185, 187
Zeus 46

If you enjoyed this book, you might also be interested in these other high-quality literary works from Arx Publishing...

Angels in Iron by Nicholas C. Prata
"The novel's principal strength is its attention to historical detail and the unrelenting realism with which the battle scenes—and there are many—are described....In addition to being an exciting action/adventure yarn and quite a page-turner, *Angels in Iron* is valuable as a miniature history lesson....This is a book that belongs on the bookshelf of every Catholic man, should be read by every Catholic boy (11 or older, I would say), and stocked by every Catholic school library."
—*Latin Mass Magazine*

Belisarius: The First Shall Be Last by Paolo A. Belzoni
"The book strikes one as a conservative rallying cry to the 'Christian West' today....Not that the book deliberately carries a political message. On its own terms, it is an ambitious tale, filled with action, spectacle, and intrigues of all kinds....Painstakingly authentic in its historical, military, and religious detail, assiduously researched and replete with facts."
—*John J. Desjarlais, CatholicFiction.net*

Leave If You Can by Luise Rinser
"Speaking of treasures, I loved *Leave If You Can*. It is a very good book to form people in an understanding of a vocation. And there are some powerful lines in it in that regard. People may think that one always is holy and attracted to religion, but that is often enough not the case. One can be called and have an aversion. That's why I think the book has a lot to teach. In that respect, it is a true story."
—*Sister Magdalene of the Hearts of Jesus and Mary, OCD*

For further information on these titles, or to order, visit:
www.arxpub.com

Also available: *The Christian Roman Empire Series*
including the following titles of interest...

The Chronicle of John, Bishop of Nikiu	The Life of the Blessed Emperor Constantine: In Four Books from 306 to 337 AD
The Ecclesiastical Annals of Evagrius: A History of the Church from AD 431 to AD 594	The Dialogues of Saint Gregory the Great
	The Complete Works of Saint Cyprian
The Life of Saint Augustine: A Translation of the Sancti Augustini Vita by Possidius, Bishop of Calama	The Fragmentary History of Priscus: Attila, the Huns and the Roman Empire, AD 430 to AD 476
The Life of Saint Simeon Stylites: A Translation of the Syriac in Bedjan's Acta Martyrum et Sanctorum	The Ecclesiastical History of Sozomen: From AD 324 to AD 425

For more information on this series, see our website at:
http://www.evolpub.com/CRE/CREseries.html

www.ingramcontent.com/pod-product-compliance
Lightning Source LLC
LaVergne TN
LVHW041332080426
835512LV00006B/422